ALSO PUBLISHED BY

BOOKS

Days in the Lives of Social Workers: 50 Professionals Tell "Real-Life" Stories from Social Work Practice, Second Edition
Edited by Linda May Grobman

Improving Quality and Performance in Your Non-Profit Organization
by Gary M. Grobman

The Nonprofit Handbook, Second Edition
by Gary M. Grobman

The Non-Profit Internet Handbook
by Gary M. Grobman and Gary B. Grant

The Pennsylvania Non-Profit Handbook, Fifth Edition
by Gary M. Grobman

The Social Worker's Internet Handbook
by Gary B. Grant and Linda May Grobman

MAGAZINE

The New Social Worker—The Magazine for Social Work Students and Recent Graduates

GUIDE TO SELECTING AND APPLYING TO MASTER OF SOCIAL WORK PROGRAMS

FOURTH EDITION

GUIDE TO SELECTING AND APPLYING TO MASTER OF SOCIAL WORK PROGRAMS

FOURTH EDITION

Jesús Reyes, AM, ACSW

Guide to Selecting and Applying to Master of Social Work Programs
Fourth Edition

by Jesús Reyes

Published by:

White Hat Communications

2001 N. Front St., Bldg. 2, Suite 325
Post Office Box 5390
Harrisburg, PA 17110-0390 USA
717-238-3787 Voice
717-238-2090 Fax
http://www.socialworker.com

ISBN: 1-929109-01-6
Library of Congress Card Number: 99-68549

TABLE OF CONTENTS

Preface

This is the fourth edition of the *GUIDE TO SELECTING AND APPLYING TO MASTER OF SOCIAL WORK PROGRAMS.* As was the case for the other editions, it is intended for anyone considering attending a graduate program in social work. This work was born out of a desire to give potential graduate students of social work a starting point and perspective to evaluate their interests and how schools may or may not meet their needs. It provides insight into how to better prepare, both through class and field experiences, for the graduate study of social work. Once those tasks are accomplished, this *Guide* serves to provide the potential graduate student of social work with information on how to best compose the application.

This is the second edition published by White Hat Communications. I am very pleased to have the publisher of *The New Social Worker* magazine handling this work. Linda Grobman, founder of White Hat Communications, is herself a social worker and shares my commitment to serving the needs of the very special population of aspirants to a career in social work. Many of the additions to the third and fourth editions were kindly suggested by Ms. Grobman. They include a "Helpful Hints" section at the end of each chapter with "Do's and Dont's" to assist readers in making the best use of the material presented as well as an "Application Tracking Sheet," to assist readers as they proceed through the application process.

This edition includes the new section, "In Their Own Words," a description of many MSW programs written by representatives of the programs themselves. This section is the result of a survey that White Hat Communications and I conducted. In this section, you will find specific tips to applicants from the 67 schools that responded. Also, they have commented on what they consider to be the most common mistakes that MSW applicants make. Also new to this edition is Chapter 14, in which I discuss applying to doctoral programs. If you are thinking of continuing your education beyond the master's level, this chapter is for you.

This edition continues to have an entire chapter on the "nuts and bolts" of writing the biographical statement, as well as worksheets to use when preparing the statement and visiting schools. Chapter 11 outlines typical questions on biographical statement instructions, as well as practical "what-is-the-question-behind-the-question" advice. This section was suggested to me by numerous readers of the previous editions.

My primary sources for what you will read in this *Guide* were the hundreds of potential applicants I met across the country during my years in recruitment at the School of Social Service Administration (SSA) of the University of Chicago. In addition, over the course of the last several years, I've had the wonderful opportunity to talk, correspond by postal and e-mail, and meet many readers of the first three editions. Their questions and commentaries were always insightful, intelligent, and challenging. Although no single person asked all the questions I address in this work, all originated with potential students. I am grateful to every one of them for their dedication and persistence in learning about our profession and how it trains its practitioners.

My colleagues at SSA as well as in other institutions across the country were equally invaluable sources. The many colleagues and mentors I've had the good fortune to know through my years in college, graduate school, and in many settings within the profession influenced much of the content of this *Guide*.

The types of graduate programs and the backgrounds of potential students vary a great deal. Through this *Guide*, you will get a sense of the variety of programs available, their possible strengths and weaknesses, and the sorts of factors to explore.

This *Guide* also presents the reader with a feel for how graduate schools approach the formidable task of sorting through the myriad of backgrounds and interests represented in each year's applicant pool. How do schools decide who is to be offered admission and who is not? How do they make an inherently subjective process work?

An understanding of how schools look at applicants will help the reader better prepare in college and through other means and to better present his (throughout this book, I refer to applicants, students, and professionals alternately as "he" or "she," since social workers come in both the male and female variety) own case for admission. Schools are genuinely invested in selecting applicants who will benefit from and contribute to the school's programs and, ultimately, to the profession and the people it serves.

Yet, schools must make decisions purely on what is contained in the applicant's file. Knowing what to highlight in a way relevant to schools can make all the difference. As a result of my experiences in this field, I am convinced that each year many applicants who would make excellent students and professionals are denied admission. Often, it is not because their credentials are lacking; rather, it is because they failed to highlight aspects of their experiences that could have made a big difference to the school.

I hope this *Guide* proves a faithful companion in your search for the right graduate program for you.

On a personal note, I express my eternal gratitude to my wife, Bobbi, for her steadfast support through the many hours I spent on this work that could have, instead, been spent with her.

Jesús Reyes, AM, ACSW

Part I

What Applicants Should Look For In Schools

What Applicants Should Look For In Schools

Most programs of social work will provide you, on request, with catalogs and brochures free of charge. All schools prepare their materials in good faith and without any attempt to misrepresent their programs or misguide the reader. Aside from their content, catalogs and brochures are useful in that they convey a sense of how the institution views itself by virtue of its choices of the aspects of its program to emphasize, general format, and photographs. Some catalogs are rich in style but lacking in substance while others, sometimes not as pleasing to the eye, are rich in content.

Some schools have more funds than others to devote to publicity materials. Usually, but not always, schools that are named after an individual (such as the George Warren Brown School of Social Work of Washington University in Saint Louis, Missouri) have added funds from endowments provided by that individual. This sometimes results in beautifully composed and produced brochures. Look beyond the workmanship of the brochure to its content. The two do not always match. In the case of George Warren Brown, however, the quality of the programs more than equals the beautifully created brochures. Whichever catalogs land in your mailbox, it is important that as a consumer, you look beyond what each school chooses to present.

Part I of this Guide *will provide you with a template for looking at social work programs. It will begin with a look at general criteria to evaluate in social work programs, including program accreditation and its implications to your ability to be licensed as a social worker, and how to interpret program rankings. Questions to ask schools about financial aid, application procedures, and factors to consider about aid will follow. The focus will then turn toward common types of academic programs (both in the classroom and in the field), dual-degree, and specialty programs and how you can assess if they meet your needs. Ways of assessing faculty background, qualifications, and interests will also be discussed, as will methods of evaluating support services such as academic and career counseling, physical facilities, libraries, computer facilities, and job placement services. Part I concludes with suggestions for assessing the achievement of alumni (by their fruits ye shall know them).*

Chapter 1

The MSW Decision

Whether you are a "first-timer" selecting your first career after college, a "career-changer" who has been in a non-social work career for a number of years, or a "career-enhancer" who has been in social service for a fair amount of time and seeking additional training in social work, the decision to seek a Master of Social Work degree merits serious thought. In a survey of current MSW students and recent graduates, *The New Social Worker* magazine found that respondents felt the best advice they could give prospective MSW applicants was to be realistic about graduate school expectations. Many emphasized the need to be ready for a more demanding academic experience than in college and to be prepared for intense field experiences.

"First-Timer" Career Seeker

For the young reader, however, the task appears particularly daunting. It is somewhat paradoxical that most of us must do something as important and with as many implications for our future as deciding on a career at a time in our lives when we may not have a great deal of "real world" experience. If you are a young person who went directly to college upon completing high school and are now contemplating going directly to graduate school, you may feel ill-prepared to make a career choice at this time in your life. It may be comforting for you to know that career changing is more likely to become the norm than the exception in our rapidly evolving world. Therefore, it is likely you will, at some point in your future, be making a career adjustment. Nevertheless, the choice of career now is important because, even though there may be career changes somewhere in your future, the *skills* you acquire in a given career ideally should be transferable to succeeding career areas. For example, social work skills such as advocacy, working across system levels, and communication are readily transferable to areas as varied as law, business management, and others.

The decision to seek a Master of Social Work degree requires careful research about the profession along with thoughtful reflection on your abilities and interests, culminating in an evaluation of the "fit" between them. In addition, it would be most useful, as much as it may be possible at this time, to consider possible alternate paths your career may take down the road. Your university career services office can assist you in evaluating your interests and aptitudes through individual advising, interest inventories, and other instruments, as well as resources to explore career options. In all likelihood, they can offer books similar to this one about other helping careers. An option to consider is to seek employment in social work or a related field and postpone graduate work until you've had the opportunity to learn more about the field, explore related options, and test your interest. Chapter 9 in this book discusses how to locate a site for gaining exposure to the profession of social work.

"Career Changer"

If you are a person who has worked a good number of years in a field unrelated to social work—in other words, a "career changer"—it would be useful to evaluate the skills you have developed in your present field and how you see those skills as forming a foundation toward a future career. The crucial general question will be whether there is a match between your goals, present skills, and social work. Can meaningful connections be made between your past work, graduate studies in social work, and future professional goals? Can the skills that you employed in the past be enhanced by social work training to achieve your goals? In short, are there specific connections between your previous experiences and education and what you hope to obtain from a graduate program to train you for practice in whatever area(s) of social work you may be contemplating?

Even though your professional experiences are outside of social work, upon graduation from a Master of Social Work program you will have more to offer an employer than the typical graduate. The challenge will be to help the potential employer see how your previous skills make you more capable to perform the job. Ask the admissions office at the graduate schools you are considering to put you in touch with alumni who came to their school as "career changers" with a similar prior background to yours. Ask them how their previous background has enhanced their abilities as social workers and, most importantly, if they are happy with their decision to change careers to social work.

"Career Enhancer"

If you have worked in the field of social work or in a related field for many years, and are contemplating seeking a Master of Social Work degree to expand your knowledge and options in the field, the decision is somewhat simpler. By virtue of your experience, you have a clearer sense, in essence, of what you're getting into. It may be possible for you to obtain financial assistance through continuing education funds through your employer. Nevertheless, it will be important for you to carefully consider the costs of investing the time and funds for a graduate education versus the personal and professional benefits of doing so. Important variables for you to consider will be your age and expected years of practice beyond graduate school.

Social Work Career Considerations

Whatever the point in your life where you presently find yourself, there are a number of characteristics about social work as a profession that are very much worth considering.

Social work highly values a systemic perspective. The social worker must have an appreciation that people exist within multiple environments and, in turn, affect and are affected by those environments. Individuals and families exist within a social environment that involves the interaction of biological, psychological, familial, economic, legal, and cultural factors. An understanding of the person-in-environment is perhaps social work's most distinguishing characteristic. Therefore, if you are someone who prefers dealing with problems that are solvable in a predictable and linear way, such as a mathematical equation, you may find it frustrating dealing with issues that may have multiple causes and equally as many possible solutions. If, on the other hand, you are stimulated by a myriad of perspectives on any given issue, you may enjoy social work. For example, the factors contributing to housing problems, and corresponding solutions, in an urban setting may be quite different from those contributing to housing problems in a rural setting.

Social work often takes place in a multidisciplinary setting. The social worker should have an appreciation of how other disciplines such as psychiatry, psychology, and law can offer much-needed insight into meeting social service needs. Important as well is the ability to work across system levels and communicate effectively with people of different disciplines. For example, a social worker in the field of social welfare might provide family therapy at one point in the day and testify as an expert witness in court later the same day. If you are a person who does not enjoy differing views and diverse settings, social work is probably not for you.

Social workers need the ability to work independently, organize multiple tasks, and have a reasonable level of frustration tolerance. The social worker often is, so to speak, the hub of the wheel of service planning and delivery. At the direct service level, she often coordinates the entire process from the point of initial referral to completion of needed services and, if appropriate, outcome assessment. At the administrative or policy-making level, social workers are at the forefront of identifying needs, formulating programmatic solutions, overseeing the implementation of programs, and evaluating programmatic outcomes. Initiative and self-motivation are important in conceiving needed courses of action for enlisting the collaboration of sources within and outside social work to facilitate change. People who enjoy predictability in their workday will often not find it in social work. People who enjoy fresh and varied challenges, on the other hand, will feel at home in the field of social work. At the same time, however, it should be noted that many of the challenges are so formidable that a solution may not be available, because of cost or other barriers. Therefore, a social worker's day often also includes frustrations associated with seeing needs that cannot be met completely, and, in some cases, not at all.

Social workers must be sensitive to the cultures represented in the service population. A lack of understanding of customs, beliefs, and behaviors of various cultures can easily result in erroneous conclusions and recommendations. An understanding of different cultures, however, can yield optimally appropriate results in that a cultural lens provides perspective and accurate meaning to observations. A person who does not appreciate differences and does not thrive in a diverse environment will find social work difficult. The social worker must be keenly aware of his own cultural bias and not allow it to form the basis of assumptions about people whose cultural background may ascribe different meanings to similar contexts. For example, communicating in a direct and blunt fashion may be valued in one culture but seen as impolite and tactless in another.

Excellent verbal and written communication skills are necessary for any social worker. Whether communicating with clients while providing counseling, with other systems while advocating client needs, or with foundations while securing support, the social worker must be able to express ideas and concepts clearly and succinctly. Tactful and clear communication skills must be exercised at all times. By the same token, the worker must possess the ability to write reports accurately and completely. For example, judges often make difficult and important decisions about parental rights and custody issues based on reports submitted by social workers.

Social workers must feel empathy for clients and their experiences. It is very likely that some, or even many, of the previous experiences with service providers were less than satisfying for the client. Therefore, the social worker often is, in essence, initially judged based on the client's previous experiences—good and bad. Making a connection that results in the client's investment in the treatment process will require overcoming whatever obstacles exist as a result of past experiences. In addition, the social worker must be aware that being in need of social services is inherently a difficult position. Whereas the social worker cannot remove all the discomforts a client experiences, the worker's ability to treat the client with respect and empathy can go a long way toward making the experience more tolerable and fruitful.

Knowledge of community resources is invaluable in assisting the social worker in identifying sources of service. Regardless of the type of service the social worker delivers or administers, clients often have multiple needs. Sources for referrals might include public and private agencies, as well as community organizations. An understanding of resources, their services, and criteria for service can help the social worker in meeting client needs. The ability to come to know, understand, and mobilize other services for clients is vital to a social worker. A social worker should enjoy networking and contacts with many people.

The characteristics listed above are certainly not the only ones useful in social work. Many of the skills, as well as the diverse knowledge base guiding the practice of social work, are not exclusive to social work; rather, social work is a dynamic profession that, from its beginnings, felt totally comfortable utilizing whatever knowledge proved useful, regardless of its origin. Therefore, social workers can be said to be generalists who interface comfortably with many professions and disciplines including psychology, anthropology, medicine, public policy, economics, philosophy, and many others. Whatever knowledge base social workers utilize, all are agents of change. Social workers are not ivory-tower observers of society; they are active agents in the shaping of society. Social work practitioners endeavor to improve the social condition for everyone. The challenges, frustrations, and rewards of a career in social work are as varied and all-encompassing as the ambitious goals of the profession.

Helpful Hints

Do...

- consider the skills you already have and how they apply to social work.
- consider how the skills you will acquire in MSW training will apply to possible future career choices.
- consider realistically how an MSW will expand your career options.

Don't...

- overlook taking advantage of vocational aptitude tests that may confirm social work is right for you or reveal other alternatives to explore.
- forget to take advantage of career advising available at your present or former college or university.
- leap into a social work degree program until you are satisfied that social work is a good fit with your personality, skills, and career goals.

Chapter 2

General Criteria for Evaluating MSW Programs

As of September of 1999, there were 132 accredited graduate programs of social work in the United States and an additional 20 in candidacy. The number of accredited programs in June of 1997 and June of 1995 were 121 and 117, respectively, while the number in candidacy were 18 and 12, respectively. The gain of 11 accredited MSW programs in the course of two years may appear modest; yet, when it is considered that an additional 20 are waiting in the wings, it is evident that the profession of social work will continue to experience a period of expansion.

The Council on Social Work Education (CSWE) has been the accrediting body for graduate and undergraduate social work programs in the United States since 1952, when it succeeded the American Association of Schools of Social Work in that role. CSWE accreditation ensures that all programs establish and maintain high standards of professional preparation for entry-level practice in the profession of social work. Please refer to Part III of this *Guide* for a complete list of CSWE-accredited graduate programs of social work. Also, see Part III for a list of Master of Social Work Programs in Candidacy and read carefully the CSWE statement on candidacy found in that same section.

As you review the curricular content of various schools of social work, you will find striking similarities. The reason for the similarities is that CSWE has six specific content areas that must be addressed by all accredited social work programs. The areas are human behavior in the social environment, social welfare policy and services, social work practice, social work research, field work, and additional requirements.

Choosing an Accredited School

As you consider schools, it is most important that you make sure they are CSWE-accredited or in candidacy for accreditation. Schools that are accredited by CSWE have gone through a rigorous process to ensure that they meet the minimum standards for social work education and that their graduates are prepared to practice social work at a professional level.

Some schools may state that they are "in candidacy" for CSWE accreditation. Candidacy is a pre-accreditation status, and schools must have met certain requirements to be admitted into candidacy by CSWE. Schools that are in candidacy are working toward accreditation and have shown that they have the potential to achieve that status. Assuming that the school completes candidacy and receives full accreditation, students who attend the school while it is in candidacy will receive accreditation of their degrees once the school is accredited, if the degree is earned under the same curriculum that receives accreditation. If you are considering a school that is in candidacy, ask when the school expects to receive accreditation and whether the curriculum you will receive your degree under is the curriculum under which the school expects to receive accreditation. (To give you an idea of the movement from candidacy to accreditation, 10 of the 15 programs listed as "in candidacy" in July 1996 are now accredited. The other five, two of which are part of a joint program between two schools, are still in candidacy.)

Having an accredited degree is important for a number of reasons. Besides ensuring that your education meets minimum professional standards, you need an accredited degree in order to receive most state social work licenses. An accredited degree will also enhance your employment opportunities, and some professional associations (such as the National Association of Social Workers) require it in order to join or receive full membership privileges.

Licensing and Certification

Being able to obtain a social work license is important because most states require a license in order to practice as a social worker. Moreover, being licensed by the state in which you practice enhances your professional credibility. A few states now allow workers with degrees other than in social work to be licensed in social work. In those states, people holding master's degrees in related fields such as guidance and counseling, family studies, and clinical psychology, among others, can sit for licensing examinations on the same basis as those holding master's degrees in social work.

Most states, however, require a master's in social work. At present, all fifty states, the District of Columbia, and the Virgin Islands allow holders of master's degrees in social work from accredited schools to be licensed or certified as social workers at a variety of levels of practice. Of those, many require a doctorate or master's in social work (none require the doctorate above the MSW), while 35 also allow licensure or certification for holders of bachelor's degrees from accredited programs of social work. Ten accept a bachelor's degree in a related field with varying amounts of social work experience. A handful of states allow certification of holders of associate's degrees, one or two years of college, as little as a basic high school education, or merely hands-on experience.

The master's degree from accredited graduate programs of social work remains the standard for professional independent practice. Most states now have multiple levels of licensure or certification. Those states that allow certification or licensure of holders of degrees other than the master's do so at levels of practice requiring only basic skills. For example, the state of Alabama reserves its highest license of Private Independent Practice (PIP) for holders of doctorates or master's degrees in social work, whereas those holding only a bachelor's in social work may only be licensed at the Licensed Bachelor Social Worker (LBSW) level. An example of certification and licensure with less than a bachelor's degree is the Registered Social Work Assistant, or SWA, in Ohio.

Even if the state in which you intend to practice allows social work licensing with a related degree, consider that we live in a highly mobile society and someday you may relocate and find yourself in a state that does not allow licensing of holders of degrees other than social work. In addition, one of the unique aspects of the profession of social work is that the master's degree is considered the terminal degree. Therefore, you can rest knowing that by obtaining a master's degree in social work, you will be in a position to practice anywhere in the country.

As mentioned earlier, no states require a doctorate in social work in order to be licensed or certified. In fact, less than five percent of holders of master's degrees seek a doctorate. Those obtaining doctorates in social work (Ph.D. or DSW) most often conduct social research or teach in a variety of settings.

Part III of this book contains a list of addresses and telephone numbers of state licensing bodies. In each state's listing, you will also find a listing of the levels of practice the state recognizes and the educational and experiential requirements for each level. The list also provides information on the category of examination required for each type of certification or licensure. The address and toll-free telephone number of the American Association of State Social Work Boards (AASSWB), which administers the exams, may also be found in the same section of this book. Check with the state or states where you may be residing in the future for their specific requirements.

In addition, some states may have other certification or licensing requirements for specific types of social work practice. One good example is the practice of school social work. In the state of Illinois, for instance, the State Board of Education must certify school social workers. Another example is California, where school social workers must hold the Pupil Personnel Services Credential. In such states, graduate students interested in school social work certification must take specific courses in the classroom and in the field as part of the master's program. Check with the licensing bodies of the states where you may be residing after graduate school about their specific requirements.

Licensing and certification of social workers vary a great deal from state to state. Most states have at least two levels of licensure or certification for holders of master's degrees in social work, though what they are called varies. The first level is available to anyone who has received a master's degree in social work (as mentioned earlier, a few states allow holders of master's degrees in related fields to be licensed as social workers). There is an exam required and, upon successful completion, licensure or certification is awarded. Illinois and Indiana, for example, call this level Licensed Social Worker (LSW).

The second level of licensure or certification that exists in most states requires two years of post-master's clinical supervised experience. Upon documentation of the experience and successful completion of the examination, licensure or certification is awarded. This level of licensure or certification is usually required for independent clinical practice. Most insurance companies and third-party payers require it for payment of clinical services. Illinois and Indiana, for example, call this level Licensed Clinical Social Worker (LCSW). Most states also have lower levels of licensure or certification for holders of bachelor's and lesser degrees.

Most state licensing and certification examinations are administered by the American Association of State Social Work Boards (AASSWB). AASSWB administers four categories of exams—Basic, Intermediate, Advanced, and Clinical. Not every state has provisions for all four categories. The Basic exam is required by most states that allow certification or licensure of bachelor's level social workers. The Intermediate, Advanced, and Clinical exams are required in most states for MSW degree holders. The examinations are objective in form and have 170 questions (20 of which scattered throughout the exam are pre-test items not used in scoring). Candidates are allowed four hours to complete an examination.

Some states have reciprocity agreements, while others do not. Therefore, if you plan to relocate sometime in the future, you may or may not need to undergo another licensing examination. In Part III of this *Guide,* you will find a listing of the type of exam required by each state. AASSWB (1-800-274-2021) can provide information on the exam required by any state and reciprocity agreements among states.

In addition to state licensing, voluntary certification is provided by the National Association of Social Workers (NASW). NASW grants the title ACSW (Academy of Certified Social Workers) to those social workers with a minimum of two years of post-master's experience and who qualify through an examination. Other professional credentials offered by NASW include School Social Work Specialist (SSWS), Qualified Clinical Social Worker (QCSW), and Diplomate in Clinical Social Work (DCSW).

Must the Diploma Read "Master of Social Work"?

Although most CSWE-accredited schools of social work grant Master of Social Work degrees, not all do so. For all intents and purposes, including the important issue of certification and licensing, it does not matter. Whether your diploma reads, "Master of Social Work," "Master of Social Service Administration," "Master of the Science of Social Work," or "Master of Arts" (all actual examples of degrees granted by CSWE-accredited graduate programs of social work in the United States), the only issue that matters is whether or not the granting institution is accredited by CSWE. The licensing agencies are not concerned with what your diploma says, but simply that it be from a CSWE-accredited institution.

In some instances, there may actually be some advantages, purely in terms of perception rather than substance, to the diploma reading something other than "Master of Social Work." There are a great many who will take issue with this point of view. I choose to offer it here simply to put it on the table and make readers aware of its existence.

For those of you who expect to practice in social policy, research, analysis, community organization, and other non-clinical areas, there may be advantages to having a degree other than the traditional MSW. Many of the people who review applicants for positions in non-clinical settings may not have a social work background. Some may not be fully aware that many graduate schools of social work have excellent training in research, policy formulation and analysis, community organization, and similar areas. Therefore, when they review a résumé that states the person holds an MSW, they may be inclined to dismiss the applicant as someone versed in clinical but not policy areas. If the résumé states something else, such as a Master's in Social Service Administration, the potential employer may be less likely to be misled.

On the other hand, clinical graduates of schools that grant diplomas other than the traditional MSW are not usually miscast as "non-clinicians," because they are eligible for clinical certification and licensing.

Let me quickly follow the above by warning you against making a choice of school simply on what your diploma will say. Most schools of social work, regardless of programmatic focus on clinical versus policy education, offer Master of Social Work (MSW) degrees. In fact, many of our nation's leading policy and administrative programs grant MSW degrees. If you find such a school that meets your needs as a policy student, don't hesitate to pursue enrollment. All it may mean down the road is that when, and if, you encounter a potential employer who has the misconception that MSW automatically means clinician, you will have to tactfully educate that person.

The reader who is extremely interested in policy issues may at this point be wondering what the advantages are of a policy education within a social work program. How does it differ from a program in public policy? In general, public policy programs tend to be broader in their approach to policy, and will be just as likely to look at a space program, for instance, as social programs. A social work-based policy program will focus only on social welfare policy.

Another typical difference is that public policy programs tend to take a quantitative approach, whereas social work policy programs tend to take a qualitative approach to the subject. Public policy programs, therefore, tend to have more extensive requirements in the area of quantitative research than social work policy programs.

Program Rankings

There are a number of rankings of graduate programs in social work and social welfare. I advise caution in letting your choice of school be driven by them. They tend to have the same bandwagon effect on some applicants that the old advertising phrase "seven out of ten doctors recommend..." has on purchasers of aspirin. Keep in mind that rankings are the end result of someone's idea of what constitutes a good program. That "someone's" ideas may be based on needs and priorities very different from your own. Beyond that, that someone's methodology for evaluating or ranking the programs may be less than perfect. Whose point of view they represent is also important.

Having made the above disclaimer, I will add that, when placed in their proper perspective, rankings can be useful. They give applicants a feel for how the school and, by extension, its graduates, are seen, at least within academe.

Rankings generally tend to be done by educators for educators and students. Just how many practicing social service professionals know the rankings or that they even exist is questionable. Those practicing professionals who are graduates of the highly ranked schools know of the rankings, because their schools tend to feature the rankings in alumni publications. On the other hand, practicing professionals outside of academe who are graduates of lower-ranked or not-at-all-ranked schools probably never hear about rankings, because their schools are unlikely to feature a story on rankings in alumni publications. The mainstream press and other media, with the notable exception of *U.S. News & World Report* (more on this later), are also unlikely to feature stories on rankings of academic programs.

If you plan to remain in academe, whether by teaching and doing research in an academic setting once you have your master's or by pursuing a doctorate, the ranking of the school you attend may be more relevant. Within academia, the rankings are analogous to the price of stocks in business. The higher the ranking, the higher the "stock." There are also, from time to time, studies on the amount of research and writings produced at various schools. Within the academic world, those reports are significant. That is the stuff that tenure is made of. Overall, the academic ranking of the program you attend may or may not assist you in securing employment.

Two well-known rankings on social work programs are worth mentioning. They are very different from one another in the methodologies they employ.

The more empirically sound of the two is *The Gourman Report: A Rating of Graduate and Professional Programs in American and International Universities* (Gourman, J., Sixth edition, Revised. Los Angeles: National Education Standards, 1993). Gourman offers rankings based on specific criteria including, among many others, the age and experience of the institution, qualifications of the faculty, curricular content, and support services and physical facilities. It offers a good starting point for those interested in programs of national prominence.

The second ranking is that of *U.S. News & World Report.* The inclusion of schools of social work in the magazine's annual education issue began in 1993 and appeared again in 1996. *U.S. News & World Report's* 1997 rankings of schools of social work may be found on the Internet at http://www.usnews.com/usnews/edu/beyond/gradrank/gbsocwrk.htm.

The methodology employed in determining rankings consisted of a survey of opinions of senior faculty and deans of schools of social work. To what extent the respondents' loyalty to the schools they attended or where they are employed played a part in their responses is anyone's guess. Given that the magazine is so widely distributed and known, the results of the survey may become widely accepted by the general public, despite the weak methodology.

Financial Aid

The levels of financial assistance vary greatly from program to program. Generally speaking, the level of aid is higher at private programs than at programs in public universities. Some state-supported institutions award little or no student aid.

Ask each school you are considering to give you figures on the amount of aid awarded the previous year's incoming class. They should be able to provide you with a range, mean, median, and mode. If the school is state-supported, it should be able to provide you with figures for in-state versus out-of-state students. Also ask for the percentage of students who receive aid.

Types of Aid

Most schools award a combination of need-based aid and merit-based aid. The former is purely based on an applicant's financial situation and what his expected income will be while a student. Generally speaking, if an applicant has not been claimed as a dependent on his parents' income tax return for the year preceding admission, the parents' income will not be considered. Ask the specific schools you are considering for their policy on parental income.

Merit-based aid is not at all based on the student's financial status but rather on the student's application rating relative to other students being admitted in the same group. The strength of the admission committee's rating is the sole determinant.

Many schools also have specialized scholarships specifically for students of color and other groups. Some have fellowship money for students admitted to certain specialty programs (refer to "Specialty Programs" in Chapter 5 of this book).

I advise students not to make their initial decision of schools to consider solely on the basis of the tuition amounts. Instead, I advise selecting schools based on their programs and their relevancy to your learning goals and professional objectives. I do believe you should include among the schools to which you make application for admission a balance between state-supported schools and private schools. Follow to the letter each school's requirements and deadlines for submission of the financial aid application.

Alternative Scholarships

Before you go to all lengths to attempt to secure outside sources of scholarships, fellowships, and alternate funding, inquire of the schools what effect outside scholarships will have on the school's award to you. Most schools will reduce their award to you by an amount equal to the outside award. The rationale is that your financial need is less as a result of the outside aid. In essence, all your extra efforts to secure outside scholarships will benefit the school instead of you.

Graduate Assistantships

If your undergraduate academic record is exemplary, a graduate teaching assistantship may be a possibility. The key determining factor will be the match of your college major and the undergraduate offerings at your graduate school and its host university. If your undergraduate major is social work and the school where you will be attending the MSW program also has a BSW program, there may be graduate assistantships available. The reason is that as a master's student with a BSW background, you may be able to assist in undergraduate (i.e., BSW) classes.

If your undergraduate major is something other than social work, there may or may not be opportunities to assist in BSW classes, because there may be a preference given to graduate assistants who are BSW holders. There may be, however, assistantship options in other parts of the host university. If the university has an undergraduate program in your major, there may be assistantship opportunities for you. For example, if your undergraduate major is in child development, there may be opportunities if the university has an undergraduate program in that field.

Not all graduate schools of social work have a BSW component. In those schools, assistantships for master's students are not available within the school simply because there are no undergraduate classes in which to assist. Assistantships in those settings are usually reserved for doctoral students who have a master's background to assist in the master's classes. Nevertheless, there may be an undergraduate program that matches your college major in the host university that may offer opportunities for you.

If there are no teaching assistantships available to you, you may want to inquire about research or other types of assistantships for master's level students. These may involve working several hours a week with a professor on a research study or other special projects.

In any case, graduate assistantships for master's students are more difficult to obtain than for doctoral students. The latter have the benefit of a broader academic background when compared to master's students. The benefits, however, merit a serious search. In state-supported schools, graduate assistantships often offer a full tuition waiver. In addition, they may include a stipend ranging from a few hundred dollars to as much as several thousand dollars per academic year. The benefits in private institutions are generally less generous, but worthwhile nevertheless.

The financial aid office of the school(s) of your interest is a good beginning point for exploring graduate assistantship options.

Applying For Financial Aid

Some schools make it more complicated than others to apply for financial aid. Some request as little as checking on the application whether or not you are interested in being considered for scholarships and loans. Other schools, on the other hand, provide you with lengthy lists of the scholarships available and their eligibility requirements. You are asked to determine from the list which scholarships you qualify for and asked to submit specific essays and other materials for each scholarship you select.

Most schools have their own scholarship, loan, and work study applications. Usually, those forms are not a part of the initial admission application packet; rather, they are provided to those applicants who accept offers of admission.

Most schools, however, use the Free Application for Federal Student Aid (FAFSA) in determining the need-based portion of financial awards. You can obtain that form at the financial aid office of your undergraduate institution or from the graduate schools where you make application for admission. The FAFSA is generally not available until late December and should be filed as soon as possible after the beginning of the year. You cannot file it earlier than January 1, because the data requested is based on your income for the year ending December 31. The FAFSA can also be submitted online. For further information, visit "FAFSA on the Web" at *http://www.fafsa.ed.gov/*.

Helpful Hints

Do...

- make sure the schools you are considering are CSWE-accredited or in candidacy for accreditation. Accreditation will determine whether or not you can be licensed as a social worker. (See Part III of this *Guide* for a listing of programs that are accredited and in candidacy.)

- check with the state or states where you may be residing in the future for their general social work licensing requirements, as well as for licensing in specific social work specialties, such as school social work. (See Part III for a listing of state licensing boards.)

- explore programs in public policy and public health and compare them carefully to MSW programs if your primary area of interest is policy.

- pursue all available forms of scholarships.

Don't...

- overlook schools whose diploma states something other than "Master of Social Work." What matters is whether or not a school is accredited by the Council on Social Work Education, not what the diploma states. Some of the finest social work programs offer degrees that say something other than "Master of Social Work."

- let a school's ranking play the most important role in your choice of school.

Chapter 3

Comparing Academic Programs

Even though all graduate programs of social work must meet certain common requirements in class and field work content in order to qualify for CSWE accreditation, each retains a flavor and mission all its own. Many of the requirements of the first year of graduate study, for instance, are very similar across programs. Yet, each school has a particular perspective that translates into the particulars of how those requirements are met. All schools have a particular perspective that can, for the sake of our discussion, be seen as being located somewhere along a continuum that ranges from a focus on the micro (clinical) aspects of social work to the macro (policy/administration) aspects of practice.

The Clinical to Policy Continuum

At one end of the continuum are schools that specifically focus on a clinical perspective. They have as their mission the training of social work professionals for the provision of direct services to individuals, families, and groups. Although programs at this end of the spectrum provide some policy-related courses in conformance with CSWE requirements, by and large the focus even in those courses is on policy as it affects clinical practice and not much beyond. There are advantages and disadvantages to this focus.

If you are specifically interested in clinical practice and intend to be a clinician throughout your career, you may want to seek this type of school. Faculty at this type of program are generally extremely well versed in the direct service aspects of social work. In addition, the variety of clinically-oriented electives tends to be broader at clinically-focused schools.

On the other hand, one point to consider is that even if at this time in your professional development you intend to be a clinician at the direct service level throughout your career, things may change down the road. You may later decide that you would like to explore other areas of social work. You may later discover an area of non-clinical practice that you did not know existed or an area may develop in the future that does not exist at this time. A strictly clinical education, as good as it may be in its own right, may not prepare you for all future options.

Even if not by your own choosing, circumstances may place you on a track away from direct practice. You may, for example, find yourself with an opportunity to be a supervisor or a program director in the same setting you may have originally entered intending to be a line service provider.

Many excellent schools that have a clinical focus also provide excellent classes in staff supervision, program management and development, budgeting, and related topics. Look for these types of course offerings in the school's catalog if you are leaning toward schools with a heavy emphasis on micro social work. You would serve yourself well by considering social program management classes in rounding out your clinical education. Many an excellent clinician has found himself in a supervisory position through unanticipated circumstances and wished he had more training in supervisory skills, program planning, and budgeting.

At the other end of the continuum are schools that focus heavily on policy aspects of social work including administration, policy analysis, research, and community organization.

Although most schools offer a clinical component, schools at this end of the spectrum are "top-heavy" on the policy side. Even with a clinical area of concentration, the selection among clinical electives will generally not be as broad as in the strictly clinical programs. The selection of classes on the social policy aspects of social work, however, will likely be quite good. What may be lacking in clinical classes will be made up by the opportunity to elect classes in social policy analysis and research, community organization, and management of social service organizations.

If you are at heart a clinician yet are attracted to schools with a fair amount of policy offerings, don't despair. If the clinical offerings are necessarily narrower because of the number of policy offerings, look at other programs and schools that may exist in the university at large. Does the university have good human development or family studies programs? If it does, are you able to enroll in those classes without extensive red tape and have the classes count for credit in the social work program?

Most schools tend to fall somewhere along the continuum between the extremes of purely clinical and mostly social policy. Looking at the relative balance (or imbalance) between specific class offerings in areas of clinical concentration versus policy concentration will give you a good clue as to where a school stands. The backgrounds of the faculty are also good clues. Does the school profess to have a good clinical program and yet have an imbalance of policy faculty over clinical faculty?

Many programs do an excellent job of providing a nice balance between the macro and micro aspects of social work, and others do not. In an era of increasing competitiveness in recruiting among schools, you should look beneath the recruiters' claims into the real substance of each school's program offerings and the training of the faculty charged with carrying out the programs.

Regardless of its place along the continuum, each school has its own particular model of education. Let's look, in turn, at how you can assess each program's strengths and weaknesses, whether you are interested in a clinical focus or policy focus.

Models of Clinical Social Work Education

Many people who enter the profession of social work do so out of a desire to provide direct services in areas such as child and family services, mental health, and related settings. Whereas all schools of social work subscribe to the social work mission of clinical service, they do so in various ways.

Some schools place a heavy emphasis on a particular theoretical model of clinical practice. Some schools have a definite bias toward, for instance, the traditional psychoanalytic models. Others, on the other hand, are more inclined to focus on behavioral, systemic or other approaches to practice. Still others offer a more eclectic array of various approaches.

My recommendation is to seriously consider the more eclectic models of clinical education. One reason is that the field changes rapidly. A heavy emphasis on one given approach may leave you unprepared for whatever changes occur in the future. Unless you have a good deal of clinical experience prior to graduate school and, based on that experience, you have a definite model that interests you, I believe a broad foundation in several approaches will serve you best in the long run.

Keep in mind that a graduate education serves its purpose best when it lays a solid foundation for future growth. It is not at all uncommon for seasoned clinicians with years of post-master's experience to seek specialized training through avenues ranging from institutes for psychoanalysis to institutes for family therapy.

Some examples of clinical concentration areas you will find among graduate programs in social work include:

- Children and Youth Services
- Social Work Practice With Families and Children
- Interpersonal Practice With Individuals, Families, and Groups
- Alcohol and Other Drug Abuse
- Social Work Practice in School Settings

- Health and Mental Health
- Social Work and the Aging
- The World of Work

In addition to concentration areas, many schools require students to select an area of practice on which to focus. Examples include:

- Casework
- Group Work
- Family Therapy

Some schools also provide selections of courses intended to develop specific professional skills such as case management, public speaking, and grant writing.

One way to determine a school's focus is to inquire about the percentage of students in a given area of concentration. For instance, in a school that offers both micro (clinical) and macro (policy/administration) fields of study concentration, it would be useful to learn the percentages of students in each area. If the number of students is fairly evenly distributed at perhaps no greater than a 60%/40% split in either direction, the program is probably fairly well-balanced.

Still another important component to explore in a clinical program is the types of field work placements available. More specifics on this important topic are discussed in Chapter 4 of this book.

Models of Macro Social Work Education

The approaches to macro social work education vary a great deal. They are often as unique as are the faculties of the various institutions. There are those programs that view social policy strictly from the perspective of social workers. In those programs, faculty are, for the most part, trained in social work. Other schools, however, have multiple disciplinary perspectives present on their faculties. Such schools are just as likely to have faculty trained in economics, public policy, public health, and law as they are to have faculty trained in social work.

The policy course offerings will be a good reflection of the faculty's training and interests. If you have particular interests in specific policy areas such as international social work policy, healthcare policy, immigration policy, or Latin American affairs, to name a few, a thorough review of the course offerings and faculty publications would serve you well.

Another important area of exploration is, interestingly enough, the offerings of other graduate and professional schools that are also part of the host university of the social work program. If the university has programs in public policy, law, international studies, business, or other areas of your interest, there may be the opportunity to round out your education outside of the social work program. Of course, you need to find out how available classes outside of the school in other areas of the university will be to you. If the given university does not have programs in the particular areas of your interest, find out if cooperative arrangements exist with neighboring institutions. If this is the case, you definitely want to explore implications to cost, financial aid, and the total number of courses required for graduation.

Examples of macro concentrations you are likely to come across in your search of a program are:

- Social and Economic Development
- Community Organization
- Management and Planning
- Fund Raising
- Research and Evaluation
- Social Welfare Administration
- Social Policy and Planning

Selecting Your Area of Concentration

An important question to ask of schools is at what point in the program will you be required to declare your selection of area of concentration (i.e., clinical with an emphasis on children and family treatment, or administrative with an emphasis on community organization).

The selection of an area of concentration is important because it will determine the emphasis of your graduate education. It should be noted, however, that it will not necessarily limit your job opportunities beyond graduation. As mentioned earlier in this book, all schools have a common core of foundation courses as required by the Council on Social Work Education. Therefore, all MSW holders, regardless of their school of graduation, have a core set of social work skills. The concentration adds a specialty to that core. For example, I was a clinical concentration student, yet I have held policy and administration positions as well as clinical ones.

Some schools do not expect students to declare a concentration until shortly before completing the program's general requirements. The strength of that approach is that students are better prepared at that point than at the start of the program to make an informed selection. By that point, the general requirements will have given students a good background and foundation in both the clinical and administrative/policy aspects of social welfare.

Other schools, on the other hand, require students to declare their concentration as early as the time of making application for admission. Inquire of those schools if it would be difficult for you to alter your selection if you should change your mind as a result of what you learn from the general requirement courses.

Whether a school asks you to declare your concentration in the application for admission or not, it should not be difficult to change your selection if you do it before your concentration phase begins or even soon after beginning work on your concentration. Most schools either ask explicitly in the application what your intended area of concentration will be or infer it from your biographical statement. The reason the information is important to the school during the application phase is that it allows the school to balance the numbers of students who expect to be in the various concentrations the school offers.

Helpful Hints

Do...

- examine where a school lies on the clinical to policy continuum.
- consider a balanced education among clinical and administration/policy choices.
- explore the real expertise of the faculty, based on their writings.
- find out at what point in the program you will need to declare a concentration.
- inquire how difficult it is to change concentrations.
- consider the school's academic relationship with other departments within the university, as well as with other universities and colleges in the area.

Don't...

- assume all schools are the same.
- assume your choice of concentration is not important.
- assume your choice of concentration is all-important.
- expect that if your area of concentration is micro practice that you will always be a clinician, or if it is macro social work that you will be limited to working as an advocate, supervisor, or administrator throughout your career.

Chapter 4

Field Work Options

The field work component will be a very important portion of your graduate education. In this book, the terms field work, practicum, and internship are used interchangeably as they often are by MSW schools. Field work allows the student to integrate class theory into practice, develop the skills and values central to effective social work practice, and develop a professional identity. The match between your individual learning goals and professional objectives and the field work site and field work instructor can either make your graduate experience challenging, fruitful, and enjoyable, or quite the opposite.

The field work instructor is usually a practicing professional who holds an MSW and several years of post-master's experience. The field work instructor is generally an employee of the host agency who supervises the intern (MSW student) in addition to his other duties. For example, an intern in a school will often be supervised by a field instructor who herself is a school social worker in that school. Graduate schools of social work, realizing the importance of the field work instructor, are generally very selective and provide training for field instructors. The field work component is a highly valued piece of a graduate social work education.

The Field Work Setting

One important factor to explore in your selection of a graduate program is the availability of practica in the setting of your interest. Most schools of social work have sites available in a variety of social service settings. Settings typically available include:

- Medical and Psychiatric Hospitals
- Residential Treatment Facilities
- Mental Health Clinics
- Planning and Coordinating Councils
- Councils on Aging
- Governmental Agencies
- Labor Unions
- Community Programs
- University Research and Demonstration Projects
- Family Service Agencies
- Corporations
- Veteran Facilities
- Courts
- Child Welfare Programs
- Correctional Facilities
- Schools
- Work Rehabilitation Centers
- Employee Assistance Programs

Most programs of social work require students to participate in two separate field work sites through the course of the master's program. A few programs require one continuous practicum in one site with phases of progressive exposure and involvement through the duration of the master's program.

An important question you should ask is whether you have the opportunity to select your field work sites or if they are assigned. Most of the schools that require two practica assign the first practicum site based on your stated interests and goals in your application, conversations with you, and/or written questionnaires completed after you have accepted the offer of admission. Most of these schools allow students to select their second practicum from a list of approved sites.

On the surface, you may feel uncomfortable with not having a choice of your first practicum. There are, however, some advantages. The first practicum, in those schools that select it for you, will probably not be what you would have chosen. In fact, it may be quite unlike anything you might have considered. Nevertheless, assuming the field work staff does a good job, it may turn out to be a very worthwhile experience.

I will tell you of my own experience my first year in graduate school as an example. I wrote in my biographical statement that I was very interested in pursuing a career in the field of family therapy, principally around issues related to behavioral problems of children. I also wrote in my field work questionnaire that I wanted to be placed in a family agency, where I would be involved in providing individual treatment to children and families.

My assigned field work site was as a public school social worker in a bilingual program. I was not pleased by my assignment, because I had no interest in ever being a school social worker. In addition, I knew the setting would not allow for family treatment. Nevertheless, I remained in that site throughout my first year of my graduate program.

Two years after obtaining my master's, I secured a position as a child and family therapist in an outpatient program of a community mental health center. A great many of my referrals came from schools, and I often needed to participate in Individual Educational Program staffings. My experiences as a school social work intern during my first year of graduate school were very helpful. Only then did I realize what a wonderful placement a school had been for my future goals.

A first-year practicum carefully selected by the graduate school's field placement staff based on your career goals can be most beneficial. It may not be your dream of dreams, but it may contribute in a very positive way to your development. It can provide you with experience in a setting you would probably not otherwise ever know, on a time-limited basis, under the protected status of student with a limited caseload and good supervision.

My own practicum experience the first year, as well as that of most students I've known through the years, was a positive one. Despite not having the opportunity to select the first practicum, most graduates state, albeit with the benefit of hindsight, that it was a worthwhile experience. A few, however, state the opposite.

What If I Need To Change Sites?

A question to explore in selecting a graduate program is the degree of flexibility in changing field work sites if the first selection does not work out. Field work directors may not want to offer details, for fear of opening the floodgates of students wanting to change sites. Nevertheless, asking the question and getting a feel for the approachability of the field work personnel is important. A few students at various institutions each year find themselves having to make up field work time in the summer as a result of not switching sites in time to fulfill required hours.

Typical Structures of Field Work Programs

The first portion of the field work experience is generally designed to provide the student with exposure to the profession and the development of a sound generalist foundation for practice. The advanced portion of the field work experience is designed to develop skills in the student's area of concentration. Examples of skills for development include those required of administrators of social welfare organizations, researchers and analysts of social programs, supervisors at the clinical or macro levels, clinicians in various settings, community and grass-roots organizers, and macro planners.

There are different models for structuring the field work component, depending on the school and whether the student is attending a full-time, part-time, advanced placement, or other program.

The most typical model for a full-time program of study consists of one field work practicum during the entire first year of full-time study and a different practicum during the entire second year of full-time study. Each year, depending on the school and the field of concentration selected by the student, field work can consist of anywhere from fifteen to sixteen hours per week (two full-time days) to twenty-one to twenty-four hours per week (three full-time days).

There are variations on the two field sites model. They include one continuous placement with increasing responsibility, block field work placements during summers, and full-time placements during selected terms of the school year.

Paid Field Placements

The vast majority of field placements do not provide a stipend. More specifically, paid first-year field placements are virtually nonexistent. There usually are, however, a very limited number of second-year field placements that provide a modest stipend.

Selecting a Field Work Site

The second practicum is generally selected by the student from a list of pre-approved sites provided by the school. The selection normally takes place late in the first year. It usually includes interviews to allow students and agencies an opportunity for mutual evaluation and selection.

A good source of information as you select your second practicum is the student, or students, placed there in the current year. Most schools have a directory of field site assignments. The second-year student who is currently at a site you are considering can give you excellent insight on the site and on the field work instructor. Don't neglect to ask the student questions about the safety of the site and its neighborhood. There may be times you attend field work after dark, and your safety may be an issue. Also ask more mundane questions, such as the variety of places nearby to eat and how much time you will usually have for meals.

There are important questions to explore in selecting your second-year field work site. How does the mission of the agency and the clientele it serves fit your goals? For example, if your goal is to work with clients from low-income communities, a field work site at a private practice setting largely serving middle-class to affluent clients would not be a good match. For a clinical student, the match between his interests and the agency's theoretical perspective will be important. A student primarily interested in a systemic approach to treatment should not select an agency with a predominantly psychoanalytic approach to treatment (unless, of course, he wants exposure to that model). For a policy student, the match between the agency's areas of focus and his own interests is crucial. A student interested in health issues will not benefit from placement in a municipal department largely responsible for urban planning.

Field work placements, particularly those in a student's final year of graduate school, frequently become full-time employment for the student after graduation. As you explore settings for your second field placement, ask yourself if the potential site is a place where you would like to work. Is the agency size such that there are likely to be openings when you graduate? If it isn't, is your work in that agency as an intern likely to bring you in contact with other agencies that may become potential employers?

Assessing Potential Field Instructors

The fit between you and the potential field work instructor can make all the difference. During your interview for your second-year field site, attempt to learn as much as possible about the field instructor in that agency. Don't have an interview with a person other than the person who will be your field instructor should you be offered and accept that particular placement. You want to get a feel for the chemistry between that person and you.

Most people who become field instructors do so voluntarily without additional pay from their agencies. Most are genuinely committed to the profession and seek to convey their knowledge to future professionals. In addition, most schools provide training for field instructors and closely monitor field sites. The case can be made, therefore, that there are no bad field instructors. There are, however, bad matches of field instructors and students, and such matches can have chaotic results.

There are a number of things you want to learn about your potential field instructor. What is that person's supervisory style? Some instructors employ a confrontational and challenging style. For instance, they might confront the student with a hypothetical situation and ask what the student would do. They might also challenge the student's methods in an attempt to have the student thoroughly explore the reasoning and possible consequences of his actions. Other instructors tend to be more supportive and do much more "hand holding." Others fall somewhere in between. None of these styles are necessarily intrinsically good or bad. The important issue is the degree of comfort you have with the potential field instructor's particular style.

Do the instructor's other duties allow for consultations at times other than scheduled supervisory times? Some instructors prefer not to be approached with questions and concerns at times other than scheduled meetings. Is your learning style such that it would be hampered by not having the instructor available as needed? Other instructors have no problem being available whenever the need arises. Which style suits you best is the important question.

How long has the person been a field instructor? If you are the first field work student the person has ever had, there may be some rookie mistakes you may be subject to (but maybe not). On the other hand, if the person has been a field instructor for a great many years, is he set in his ways and not very flexible?

What other specialized training does the instructor have? For a student interested in family therapy, for instance, it would be beneficial to have a field instructor with post-graduate training in family treatment. For a student interested in health administration, a field instructor with a certificate in this field would be an excellent match.

Additional Field Work Factors to Consider

There are additional questions related to field work that you may want to explore. An important item is the mechanism for communication between the school and the practicum agency. At some schools, the instructor for the methods class is also assigned the role of field liaison for the students in his class. At other schools, there is a full-time staff person fulfilling liaison duties. The liaison function is important because it monitors the quality of field work experiences. It also intervenes should any problems arise. If the mechanism is a slow one, precious time will be lost should the need arise for alternate placement. The delay could result in the postponement of the student's expected graduation date.

Another item that may be worthy of exploration, depending on your interests, is the possibility of doing a block full-time placement in the summer between years in lieu of your second-year practicum. Most schools require that practica take place concurrently with class work during the academic year. The reason is a sound one, particularly for clinical students. There is a better opportunity to apply class theory to the field and vice versa if the two are taking place simultaneously.

Some schools, however, allow students to do summer block placements. Some even allow them in cities other than where the school is located. For instance, in its 1994-96 catalog, the Wurzweiler School of Social Work of Yeshiva University in New York City lists participating field work sites in twenty states, four Canadian provinces, and in Israel and Taiwan.

You may also want to inquire if the program allows students to find their own field work sites over and above the options provided by the school, especially if you have a unique area of interest. Through the course of your first year, you may come to know of a setting that matches your interests and goals. Will the school work with you and that agency in arranging your second practicum? The potential site will still need to meet the requirements of the school in terms of the qualifications and level of experience of the field instructor, the type of supervision that must be provided, the caseload assigned an intern, and agreement to other school guidelines. I located my own field work site for my second year of graduate school, and it was a great experience. Other students have successfully created their own practica in sites not previously approved by their schools.

Helpful Hints

Do...

- explore the variety of field work settings each school offers.
- ask to what extent you have a role in determining your field work placements.
- ask how difficult it is to change field work sites if things don't work out.
- ask if there are paid field placements available (probably not too many, but worth asking).
- explore the match between your goals and experiences at the setting.
- ask if the agency is likely to have job openings when you graduate. If it isn't, is your work in that agency as an intern likely to bring you in contact with other agencies that may become potential employers?
- explore the possibility of a summer block placement.

Don't...

- underestimate the importance of the field work component to your graduate education.
- dismiss varied experiences in field work settings. They may open your eyes to new possibilities.

(continued on next page)

(continued from previous page)

- neglect the opportunity to have an interview with the person who will be your field instructor, so you can assess the "chemistry" between the two of you.
- feel it is inappropriate to ask the instructor about her supervisory style, flexibility in supervision, and other characteristics.

Chapter 5

Special Issues

There may be special issues you will want to consider when looking for a school of social work. If you are currently employed and wish to continue working, you may be interested in a part-time MSW program. If your undergraduate degree is in social work, you may qualify for advanced standing. If your career goals are very specific or unique, there may be a joint degree or specialty program that will help you meet those goals. Finally, the faculty of a particular school may have special expertise in a particular area of practice that is of interest to you, and this may influence your decision.

Part-Time Programs

An increasing number of graduate schools of social work across the nation are offering part-time programs. The Council on Social Work Education requires that students of part-time programs meet the same requirements as full-time students. The differences between full-time programs and part-time programs lie not in content and requirements, but in their structures. Therefore, everything in this *Guide* regarding classroom and field requirements applies to part-time programs as well as full-time ones. Normally, part-time programs take three years or more to complete, whereas full-time programs are usually two years in duration.

The availability of classes during off-work hours varies greatly from program to program. Some programs allow students the option of attending classes either during the day or evenings, but have a complete course of offerings that allows part-time students to complete all their required class work in the evenings.

Be aware, however, that the choices of electives in these programs may be more limited than in the day program. After all, there are simply fewer evening hours than day hours to schedule electives. It may not be cost-effective for a school to schedule a highly specialized elective at two different times, given that the total number of students taking the course is low. If you have the option of taking electives in other departments and schools of the university, explore whether those programs hold classes in the evening.

Some part-time programs offer classes during the evenings and weekends. Still others require at least a portion of the required classwork to be done during the day on Monday through Friday. Will your employer allow you the flexibility to attend day classes occasionally if the need arises?

The option of completing field work requirements during off-work hours also varies greatly among programs. Some are able to arrange field sites totally in the evenings or in some combination of evenings and weekends. The options for field sites in those programs, however, may be a great deal more limited than in day full-time programs. This is particularly true for students in administrative and policy concentrations of study. Most administrative and policy agencies do not have evening and weekend hours, so the choices are extremely limited. For clinical students, on the other hand, choices are much broader, because most clinical programs have evening hours to accommodate their clients.

It is for those reasons that a great many part-time programs do not offer the field work portion on a part-time basis. Rather than restricting their students to an extremely limited pool of field work options, those programs opt to require students to do a full-time block field placement over the course of several weeks or to do a placement several full days per week for one or more scholastic terms. The issue of your employer's flexibility as to your work hours should be settled before you apply to a graduate program and accept an offer of admission.

Some programs allow part-time students who are employed in social service settings to do one of their required internships at their place of employment. Normally, requirements include that the practicum be in a program other than the one in which the student is employed. For example, if you are employed as a medical social worker in a hospital, you may be able to do your practicum in another department of the hospital such as the outpatient adult psychiatric unit, the substance abuse unit, or another unit different from the one in which you currently work.

Another requirement may be that the person who acts as your field work supervisor be someone other than the person who is your job supervisor. In addition, that person must hold a master's degree in social work and meet the school's requirements of post-master's experience. The employer must agree to other school regulations.

The rationale for these and other requirements schools may have in allowing you to have a practicum at your place of employment is two-fold. One is that it is important that your roles as an employee and as a student be clearly differentiated. The other is that your practicum should provide a worthwhile learning experience, rather than reiterating what you already know from your job. Otherwise, you could simply end up working additional hours doing what you normally do in your job, learning nothing new, and not being compensated for the extra time. Check with the schools of your interest regarding this option and their requirements.

There are other queries you should make in exploring part-time programs. In an era of increasing financial pressure from their host institutions to be self-supporting, many schools of social work have recently entered the part-time market.

There are financial reasons that motivate schools to develop part-time programs. One is that part-time students who are employed often qualify for less financial aid from the school because they have income from full-time employment or because their employers offer tuition assistance. Inquire of the school to what extent financial aid is based on merit (the strength of your application relative to others offered admission in your group) and on need (your family income). If financial aid is based mostly on need, chances are your award will be minimal to non-existent, because you will have income from your employment.

Unfortunately, some schools have not fully considered accommodations to meet the special needs of students in the newly developed part-time programs. The hours of operation of their library, computer facility, or even dining facilities, for instance, may not have been expanded to adjust to the needs of students who are employed during the day. Administrators may still be on a nine-to-five schedule and unavailable to evening students for questions on registration, class selections, and financial aid.

Inquire about those issues before making application and considering accepting an offer of admission. As someone employed full time, attending classes part time, and attending field work part time, in addition to your personal responsibilities and commitments to your family and significant others, you already have enough on your plate. Having to wrestle for basic services with school officials will be an added burden worth avoiding.

Another factor to explore is that of the faculty who teach in the evening program. Many schools employ part-time instructors to teach in the evening program. Their regular full-time faculty may be involved only marginally, or not at all, in evening classes. Part-time faculty may or may not be capable of delivering the same level of education as full-time faculty. On the other hand, part-time faculty at some institutions may actually be much more connected to the issues of actual practice than full-time faculty, who may be primarily involved in writing and research. In addition, the availability of part-time instructors for student contact outside of class may be very limited.

Advanced Standing Programs

A great many graduate schools of social work offer advanced standing to incoming students who hold a Bachelor of Social Work (BSW) degree from an undergraduate program accredited by the Council on Social Work Education (CSWE). The number of credits granted vary anywhere from approximately the equivalent of one semester to an entire year. Therefore, it is possible for holders of a BSW to earn a Master of Social Work in as little as only one academic year of study beyond the BSW.

Schools with advanced standing programs typically reserve only a portion of spaces in an incoming class for advanced standing students. Competition for those spots among aspiring advanced standing applicants is very stiff. The mean undergraduate GPA of accepted advanced standing students is often higher than that of the conventional incoming class. If you are considering making application as an advanced standing student, seek that data from the institution so you can assess your chances realistically.

If you apply seeking advanced standing, many schools will consider you only on that basis. That is, if you are denied admission into the advanced standing program, your application will not be considered for the regular program. That means that if you are denied advanced standing, your only remaining option to enter the same school's regular program is to reapply the following year as a conventional student. Check with the schools you are considering on their policies.

Some schools do not have an advanced standing program in terms of reducing the number of total classes a student will be required to take in order to graduate. Instead, a student may waive some required courses but will need to take other more advanced courses in their place. In those programs, it is possible for students holding a BSW or related degrees such as psychology, family studies, human development, and others to request to waive out of some of the graduate program's required courses. Graduate courses typically eligible for waiver are Human Behavior in the Social Environment (HBSE) and Research and Statistics in the first year's requirements.

Typically, if the waiver request is approved after reviewing the content of similar undergraduate classes, the student is required to take other graduate courses in the place of the waived courses. Some schools offer an advanced HBSE course that must be taken if the regular HBSE class is waived, while other schools allow students receiving waivers to take elective courses of the student's choice. Therefore, the length of the program is not shortened. On the other hand, the student's education is enriched because redundancy in courses is eliminated while exposure to more advanced courses is increased.

Other schools do not have an advanced standing program at all. There is a school of thought that believes it is a disservice to the student and to the profession to rush a student through a master's program in only one year. It is believed an advanced standing student's education suffers because he does not have the benefit of the first year's practicum to lay a foundation for the advanced practicum. Rather, the advanced standing student goes directly into the advanced practicum in his only year in graduate school.

If you are leaning toward obtaining your MSW via an advanced standing program, one possible way to increase your preparation for the advanced practicum is for you to take some time to work full time in human services before going on to graduate school. Without this added experience, the advanced standing program student who goes directly from high school to college to an advanced standing program is at a clear disadvantage. Check with the schools you are considering for their policies on the maximum time allowed between earning a BSW and acceptance into their advanced standing programs. Some allow for a maximum time of five years and others have more strict standards.

The advanced standing program student must select an area of concentration right away because he will bypass most, if not all, of the program's general requirements, which are normally fulfilled before work on the selected area of concentration begins. Thus, he will not have the benefit of further exposure to, and exploration of, various aspects of social work that comes about during the general requirement phase of studies.

It can be argued that students who declare a selection of area of concentration after undergoing the general requirements phase do so in a much more informed way. Keep in mind that some schools, however, require all students to declare their area of concentration as early as the time they make application for admission.

The prime advantage of the advanced standing concept, of course, is that up to a year of school is saved for the student. If time is very much of the essence for you, you may want to consider it. On the other hand, you may also want to weigh what you will lose. Attending a conventional graduate program will allow you the opportunity to be exposed to a great deal more. The ultimate result, I believe, will be a better experience for you.

Joint Degree Programs

A good number of accredited graduate programs of social work offer joint degree opportunities. Most common offerings include joint programs with schools of law, schools of divinity, schools of business, schools of public or health policy, schools of gerontology, schools of urban and regional planning, schools of education, and others. There are also a few programs available in less traditional areas, such as dual degrees in social work and dance therapy, for instance. If you are interested in these possibilities, you have your job cut out for you. You should undertake a thorough investigation of the other program in whichever discipline you choose as carefully as you are exploring the social work program.

Applicants for admission to joint degree programs are normally required to apply to each school independently. A crucial factor in the admissions decision will be the degree to which the applicant makes a case for seeking the two degrees. How have the applicant's background and experiences in both fields tested and shaped her interests? How will the applicant's future professional plans benefit from dual training? Normally, an applicant must meet the individual entrance requirements of both programs.

There are a number of factors to consider about joint degree programs. Foremost is the fit between the two programs of study. Chances are that a number of one program's required courses will be counted as electives by the other program and vice versa. That means that you will not have as many electives in either program as non-dual degree students. You need to consider what you will be missing. If the two programs are highly complementary, the loss is minimal versus the time you save.

Joint degree programs normally save time for the student versus pursuing each program separately. For example, an MBA/MSW joint program might take three academic years of full-time study to complete. Were the two programs to be taken separately, each would take two years for a combined total of four years. Having some courses count for both programs is how the compressed time period is achieved.

Another factor to consider is whether splitting your time between two programs of study will allow you enough exposure outside of the classroom to the faculties of the two schools. A very important part of a graduate education rests on the mentoring relationships you will develop with faculty. If the two programs share some of the faculty, these relationships may be enhanced.

The source of your financial aid will vary depending on how much time you are enrolled in each program. For example, if two thirds of your classes are in program A and the other third in program B, your financial aid will probably be prorated accordingly. How will this affect your financial aid packet? If the two programs have fairly similar financial aid policies, there may not be much of an impact. If one has a much lower level of financial aid, you may need to consider additional employment or other sources of funds during the periods of time the majority of your coursework is in the program with the lower level of aid.

The best source of information is current students. Ask to be put in contact with students who are currently in the joint degree program you are considering.

Specialty Programs

In addition to joint degree programs, many schools offer specialty programs. Whereas these types of programs do not generally offer a degree in addition to the Master of Social Work, many offer a certificate that, depending on the nature and reputation of the specialty, can be very valuable. Beyond the specialty program's inherent benefits to your knowledge and professional development, a certificate can be a nice addition to your résumé, because it is an added credential.

Specialty programs are offered in a variety of areas, such as urban practice, health administration and policy, rural practice, practice with populations of color, lesbian-gay-bisexuals studies, family support, multiethnic practice, Jewish communal service, maternal child health, Native American studies, international social welfare, aging, and other specialty areas.

At some schools, there are special application procedures to participate in a specialty program. In addition, there may be a fellowship attached for each of your years of study. Normally, once the next academic year's incoming class is selected, additional information on specialty programs and special application procedures are sent to incoming students.

Advantages to participating in a specialty certificate program include the specialized and usually state-of-the-art training, the additional credential, exposure to faculty in your particular area of interest, and, in some cases, fellowship funds. You should inquire, however, if receiving additional funds through the fellowship will decrease the need-based portion of your financial aid. If fellowship funds reduce other aid by the same amount, you've really not gained any funds.

There are a number of possible disadvantages to participating in specialty programs. One is that you usually will have few to no elective classes. The classroom portion of a regular master's program usually consists of the courses in general requirements, courses in a specific area of concentration, and electives. Because of requirements of the Council on Social Work Education, students in specialty programs still have to fulfill the school's general requirements and the requirements for their selected area of concentration. Therefore, the courses of the specialty program usually take the place of the electives. If the specialty program is a good match with your interest, you will not lose by giving up electives.

If, on the other hand, you are considering a specialty program more for the possible additional funds than for the program content itself, think again. You are only in a master's level social work program once, and you want to make full use of the resources that will help you achieve the growth you will need to practice in the social work field of your choice. Whatever financial aid you may gain will be more than offset by your missed opportunities of elective courses if the specialty program doesn't truly match your interests and goals.

Faculty

The composition of the faculty also brings specific qualities to a school and how it approaches the business of educating its students. Whether you are interested in micro or macro social work, a critical issue will be the match between the type of training you are looking for and the faculty's interests and levels of experience. Explore carefully the training, background, and experiences of the faculty. Most schools include in their catalogs a list of faculty and their research interests and recent publications.

Investigate the school's faculty-student ratio. However, look also into the percentage of faculty normally on sabbatical or teaching only a part-time load or not at all as a result of research and writing commitments. The de facto faculty-student ratio may be substantially different from the reported ratio.

Does the composition of the faculty and activities reflect the school's stated mission? Most schools have beautifully crafted mission statements that speak eloquently about service to the underrepresented and vulnerable of our society. Yet, there is sometimes a discrepancy in what a school says and what a school does. Is the faculty involved in projects to serve surrounding communities through service as consultants or agency board members? To what extent does the school support faculty, students, and staff in community involvement?

If you are considering schools in cities you do not know, ask what percentage of the faculty live in the immediate area around the campus. The answer will be a good measure of the quality of the neighborhood's safety and general environment.

Does the faculty as a group represent the populations social workers are pledged to serve? Much has been written as of late about the wonders and benefits of "diversity." It has become a fashionable word to include in school catalogs and curricula. Yet, many of the schools most often quoting the concept lack diversity in their own faculty and administration.

Regardless of our level of training, experience, and expertise, our perspective is colored by our cultural lens. It is a most important part of a social work education to have the benefit of exposure to perspectives of faculty of various cultural backgrounds and sexual orientations. By the same token, it is important to have genuine diversity among the administrators who set policy on issues of curriculum and student services, including admissions and levels of student financial aid.

Another of the great benefits of a graduate education is the opportunity to interact with faculty beyond the classroom. How available are faculty to informal exchange with students, whether or not the given student is enrolled in their classes?

Those of you particularly interested in attending a school where faculty are heavily involved in ground-breaking research and publishing need to be particularly inquisitive. You may see in a school's catalog the name of a faculty person whose writings have inspired you during your undergraduate years. You will do well to ask how much actual teaching that person does. You may also want to ask how available that person is to discussions with students beyond the classroom.

Major schools are in intense competition with one another as to the percentage of faculty who publish in a given year. Therefore, some of each school's most notable faculty may be involved only marginally in actual teaching. Some notable faculty take one- or two-year sabbaticals on occasion to pursue research and writing. Will the faculty of your interest be available at the school for teaching and other contact with students during the time of your graduate education? A name on a catalog's faculty listing won't do you much good if you never actually meet the person.

It is also important to know who actually teaches the classes. Do the professors on the faculty list actually teach the classes, or are classes conducted by doctoral students? I am not at all stating that your education will not be served well by doctoral students. Many are very knowledgeable, have outstanding abilities to convey class material, and are very committed to their students. Nevertheless, you need to know what to expect, so you can develop an informed opinion about the school.

A related question is relevant to those who will be attending evening or other alternative programs. Is the faculty that teaches in the full-time program the same faculty that teaches in the alternative program? You may have been attracted to the school because of its renowned faculty and find once you are there that your classes are taught by adjunct part-time instructors. Once again, let me make clear that I am not stating that teaching by adjunct part-time faculty results in an inferior education. In fact, an argument to the contrary can be made, because many part-time instructors work during the day in real-life social service settings and bring vast practice experience to the classroom. Again, the issue is your ability to arrive at an informed decision about the school.

Helpful Hints

Do...

- ask if the part-time program will require any full-time work, such as a day field placement.
- ask if all courses in the part-time program are available in the evenings or weekends, or if you will need to take some courses during business hours to meet graduation requirements.
- ask if library and other support services are available evenings and weekends.
- ask if admissions requirements are more selective for advanced standing programs than for conventional programs (they probably are).
- consider joint-degree programs if your plans include a second degree. They can be time-savers.
- explore carefully the training, background, and experiences of the faculty.
- investigate the school's faculty-student ratio.
- ask what percentage of the faculty live in the immediate area around the campus. The answer will be a good measure of the quality of the neighborhood's safety and general environment.
- inquire about the racial and ethnic diversity of the faculty. Many of the schools that most often sing the praises of diversity lack it in their own faculty and administration.

(continued on next page)

(continued from previous page)

- check how available faculty are for informal exchange with students, whether or not the given student is enrolled in their classes.
- ask who actually teach the classes. Are they taught by faculty members or graduate assistants?

Don't...

- assume the faculty in the part-time program are the same as that of the full-time program.
- if given the option, assume that doing a field work placement at your full-time place of employment is the best option.
- assume going part-time will result in less graduate expense. With a full-time income, you may qualify for less gift aid.
- assume advanced standing programs, because they save time, should be your first choice.
- assume that if you apply for advanced standing and are rejected that you will automatically be considered for the conventional program.
- apply for a specialty program simply because it may offer additional aid.
- assume you will have access to well-known faculty. They may not be teaching or may be on sabbatical.

Chapter 6

Support Services for Students and Graduates

An important area that is often overlooked by students while exploring schools is that of support facilities and services. Good support facilities and services can make your time in graduate school more enjoyable and fruitful. Some support services, such as career placement, can make a big difference to your success when you graduate and throughout your career. Poor support facilities and services, on the other hand, can have a very negative impact on your graduate life and career.

Visiting The School

I strongly advise against making a final decision about a school without a site visit. I've visited a number of nationally ranked schools that have extremely poor physical facilities lacking, in some instances, basics such as adequate heating and cooling capabilities. Don't underestimate the impact of discomfort on your ability to concentrate on school work.

With proper notice, most schools' admissions offices can make arrangements for you to sit in on classes and meet with students and faculty during your visit. Ask to meet with students from similar backgrounds and circumstances as you. If you are married and will have small or school-age children, for instance, speaking with a current student about child care, schools, and other similar issues will be helpful. If you are from a small community and the school is in a large city, speaking with a student from a similar background about adjustment and safety issues will be beneficial.

Think of your visit as a test drive of the school. You certainly wouldn't buy an automobile without a test drive. The monetary and time investment in your graduate education is certainly much greater, and its impact on your future longer lasting, than any car you will ever purchase.

Are the classrooms and seating comfortable? Are they adequately heated or cooled? Is the school accessible to the physically disabled? Even if you do not have a disability, it is important to know. You may suffer an injury while a student that places you in a wheelchair during a period of time (it happens!). Even if the chances of your personally having even a temporary disability are remote, the fact that a school has, or doesn't have, provisions for the disabled says something about a school. It speaks to its commitment to various populations and much more.

Safety

Another important issue is that of safety. What provisions are made for the safety of students? Depending on the schools you are considering, their locations, and how familiar you are with the neighborhoods and cities, safety may or may not be a concern. If you are considering schools in major cities that you are unfamiliar with, talk to current students at the schools.

Have any students been victims of crimes on campus? Some university police departments issue weekly or monthly crime alerts detailing the locations and nature of recent incidents on campus. What provisions does the university take to safeguard its students? Some schools have free van or bus service for students to and from their dormitories and apartments during certain hours of the night. If you are thinking of living off campus and will not have a car, ask about the safety and reliability of public transportation.

Getting your social work education in a large city has some advantages. Large urban areas make excellent laboratories for the student of social welfare. They often have a wide array of cutting edge social service programs that can be excellent practicum sites.

You need to weigh those benefits against the risks of higher crime normally associated with large urban areas.

Library Services

Another area to look into is that of library services. Does the school have its own library? If it does, how well-stocked is it with books and periodicals? Is there a full-time librarian and other qualified staff available during all operating hours? Do the library's operating hours match those of the building? An open building with a closed library is of limited use. Is there electronic access to library materials?

If the school does not have its own library, how well-stocked is the university's main library with social work matter? What other school or program libraries are available to you? If your area of interest is clinical, a good psychology library on campus will be very useful. If your interests lie in policy, is there a public or health policy library available to you on campus?

Does the library have cooperative arrangements with other universities for sharing materials? If so, how long does it take to actually receive materials from sister libraries? Even better, do the libraries have state-of-the-art computers that allow you to access materials from other libraries online?

Computer Support

Does the school have its own computer center available for student use? Are its hours adequate and accessible to you? What is the technical support at the center? Is it staffed all of the time or only part of the time by qualified personnel who can meet your needs? How current are the computers and related equipment? What mechanisms are in place to keep it current?

If you have your own computer, you may want to investigate the compatibility of the school's computers and your own. Compatibility would allow you the flexibility to transport your data on disk and work on it either at home or at the school.

If you are planning to buy a computer, also ask about compatibility. In addition, inquire if the university has a computer store that offers reduced prices to students. Some, but not all, university computer stores easily beat even the lowest retail computer prices. It still pays off to comparison shop.

It may also be possible to obtain a low-interest student loan for the purchase of your computer. After all, it won't be often in your post-student life that you will obtain such favorable interest rates.

Housing

Some schools have housing on campus, while others do not. On-campus university housing usually consists of graduate dormitories and, in most instances, also graduate apartments. The quality of housing varies a great deal.

Therefore, I strongly recommend asking to view dorms and apartments. Some are new and very well-equipped with appliances, other furniture, and air conditioning. Others are nothing less than Spartan. Depending on the school's location, rents can be quite high. If you are from a relatively small community and the school is in a large urban area such as Chicago, Los Angeles, Boston, or New York City, the costs may astound you.

The same can be said about off-campus housing. School catalogs usually have an estimate of living expenses for single and married students, breaking down the typical costs of room and board, health insurance, books, local commuting expenses, and other miscellaneous expenses.

Bookstores

The cost of textbooks is higher than ever and expected to soar even higher. Whatever steps you can take to minimize textbook expenses will be helpful to your budget. Visit the university bookstore and evaluate its prices. Typically, university bookstores are at the high end of the price spectrum.

Inquire about alternative stores. Some universities have independent cooperative bookstores on or near campus that allow you to buy stock at minimal rates (perhaps $15 to become a member). Once you are a member, you can enjoy anywhere from ten to fifteen percent off the regular prices (which are usually less than university stores). Once you leave school, you can sell your stock back to the store and recover your investment with accrued appreciation.

Another alternative is to shop at online bookstores. General bookstores (Amazon.com, Barnesandnoble.com, and Borders.com, among others) sell virtually every book in print. Others, such as Textbooks.com and ecampus.com, specialize in textbooks and offer used books and buyback options. You can shop and compare prices at these bookstores at any time, day or night.

Health Services

Most of the larger universities have comprehensive outpatient and inpatient health services for students. Other universities have arrangements with local healthcare providers. Most schools require students to carry health insurance and waive the requirement to buy the university's coverage for students who show proof of alternative coverage. Still other schools require all students to pay a health fee to cover most types of outpatient services but will waive the requirement to purchase university major medical coverage with proof of alternative coverage. Costs and requirements vary greatly among schools, and it is best to make individual inquiries.

Other Facilities

Miscellaneous other facilities worth evaluating during your campus visit include dining facilities and their prices; recreational facilities, including athletic fields, swimming pools, and whatever other activities interest you; and community offerings such as museums, concert facilities, theaters, and other entertainment. The option of enjoyment can bring a nice balance to the academic challenges of a graduate education.

Advising Services

The availability and accessibility of advising services can play a critical role in your ability to get the most out of your graduate education. By and large, the first third or so of your graduate education will involve few decisions. During that period of time, your classes will be predetermined by requirements of the Council on Social Work Education. Your first field practicum will probably be assigned to you, as discussed in Chapter 4.

It is only after you begin working on your selected area of concentration that you will have choices to make in terms of class selection. Later in your first year, you will probably also have the important task of selecting your advanced practicum.

It is from that point forward that you will need knowledgeable and accessible advice. Will there be advisors within the school with backgrounds in social work to inform your decisions?

One model for advising used by schools is to divide students among faculty. Faculty are then required to serve as advisors to their assigned students. One weakness of this model is that the levels of commitment on the part of faculty to the role of advisor will vary greatly. In addition, unless a conscientious effort is made to match student and faculty interests, a given faculty person, even if invested in assisting his advisees, may not have the needed expertise.

In actual practice, many students in schools that employ that model simply seek advice independently from faculty and administrators they've come to know as sharing interests. If the school allows the flexibility, the system works. If there isn't the flexibility, the system is haphazard at best.

If there are not advisors within the school, will you have to resort to advisors at the university level who may or may not know and understand social work? Advisors at the university level are usually generalists who must advise students in numerous disciplines. Some are very knowledgeable about social work, while others have only superficial knowledge of our profession.

Job Placement Services

In the long term, the school's job placement services may be one of the most important factors to consider. As complicated and time-consuming as it is to do justice to selecting the right program for your studies, it is most important not to neglect this aspect of your search.

Some schools have job placement services of their own, while others rely on the university job placement office to provide services to students, soon-to-be graduates, and alumni.

At one end of the spectrum are those schools (not many, unfortunately) that have a full-time job placement director with a good support staff. Those schools generally provide a comprehensive range of services to social work students seeking part-time and summer employment; students about to graduate and seeking their first post-master's full-time job; and alumni exploring changes, reentering the job market, or seeking information on licensing and continuing education.

Services afforded students in schools with the in-house comprehensive model of job placement include assistance in locating part-time jobs within the university or elsewhere in research and demonstration projects. While a graduate student, I was fortunate to have a twenty-hour per week position in a university demonstration project aimed at the reduction of gang violence. In addition to supplementing my extremely tight budget, the experience was very beneficial.

A well-staffed and well-operated job placement office may also have very good files on fellowship opportunities, such as the Presidential Management Internship and paid summer internship opportunities.

This type of job placement office may also provide comprehensive training to students on job search skills, including résumé and cover letter writing, salary negotiation, interviewing skills, and self assessment as they apply specifically to the profession of social work. It may also be involved in the aggressive solicitation of job listings and on-campus interviews by local, regional, and national employers. It might also hold an annual or semiannual Career and Jobs Day and publish a printed or online jobs bulletin on a regular basis.

At the other end of the spectrum are graduate programs that rely solely on the job placement office at the university level for all their job placement needs. With increasing budgetary constraints across academe, this model may become more and more prevalent. The strength of the model for the university is that centralized services are more cost effective. The primary weakness is that the specialized needs of social workers may fall between the cracks. Nevertheless, some university job placement offices have counselors on staff who are very knowledgeable about social work and do an excellent job on behalf of social work students and alumni.

Some schools fall somewhere between the two ends of the continuum of comprehensive services housed at the school and no services at all housed at the school. They may have some services at the school level, including perhaps individual career counseling, but rely on the university office to provide social work students with generic job search skill training applicable to many disciplines.

The extent to which the school provides job services to alumni should be explored. Most schools are smart enough to realize that it makes financial sense to provide services to alumni, because happy alumni tend to make larger and more frequent gifts to schools. A good job placement office is available fully to alumni free of most charges, with the possible exception of minimal subscription costs to cover the cost of producing and mailing jobs newsletters and similar items.

Continuing Education Program

Determine if the school has a continuing education program. The extent to which a school offers its resources to practicing MSW professionals is a good measure of that school's commitment to improving the quality of social services in its own community and beyond.

As mentioned earlier in this *Guide,* your education will be far from over once you attain the Master of Social Work degree. Whether your professional focus is on policy and administration or on direct service, you will need to update your knowledge base frequently. Continuing education offers the opportunity for learning the latest approaches to the professional challenges that you will face. In addition, the opportunity to interact with other professionals by means of a workshop or seminar can be a rewarding experience that can serve to renew your professional outlook. Remember the old adage, "Take care of yourself so you can take care of others."

If you intend to practice clinical social work, the need for continuing education takes an added practical quality. Most states now require Licensed Social Workers (LSW) and Licensed Clinical Social Workers (LCSW) to submit evidence of a specified number of continuing education hours per year at the time of application for license renewal. The number of continuing education hours each state requires varies.

If the schools you are considering have a continuing education program, ask if the courses are approved to be applied toward continuing education licensing requirements in your state. Also, ask if alumni of the school are eligible for a discount when enrolling in the school's continuing education programs. Over the course of your professional career, savings can add up to a great deal.

If the school has a continuing education program, ask if students in the MSW program can enroll in workshops or seminars. Generally, such courses are not counted toward degree requirements, but a few schools are flexible enough to allow students to obtain some form of credit toward the MSW by taking continuing education classes.

Whether or not you obtain credit toward your MSW, continuing education courses can be a valuable addition to your professional growth. For example, a good one-day workshop on grant writing can be a valuable experience for anyone contemplating that sort of work. Does the school provide a discount to current MSW students who choose to enroll in a continuing education class? Some schools offer as much as fifty percent off to their students.

It may seem premature now to be thinking of continuing education courses. After all, you are only at the stage of selecting and applying to MSW programs. Yet, if you make your school selection based on a thorough understanding of what it can and cannot offer you down the road, your post-MSW relationship with your future school can be very fruitful.

Alumni Involvement

Another very effective method for schools to provide job placement services to their students, soon-to-be graduates, and alumni is to enlist the assistance of the school's alumni association. The judicious and selective use of alumni mentoring networks can yield large dividends to the school in terms of cost-free volunteer assistance and for job seeking students and alumni in terms of valuable contacts and job leads.

Another excellent use of alumni is in the provision of individual and group mentoring opportunities for providing real-world visions of career options to students. Ask the schools you are considering about the extent of alumni involvement with students. If you will be relocating upon graduation or at another time, will the school provide you with directories of alumni residing in that area? They can be valuable sources for job leads and general information about the area.

On the other hand, beware of schools that attempt to have alumni provide services that only a full-time staff should provide. Although committed and well-intentioned, alumni are volunteers who have their hands full at their places of employment. They cannot be expected to provide job services and the like without adequate support from paid staff of the school. In our current economic climate, schools may try to trim their budgets by placing unrealistic expectations on their alumni.

Remember also that you will someday be an alumnus/a. If the school shows a tendency to overuse alumni, you may be on the receiving end of that down the road. On the other hand, judicious use of alumni as resources can be very satisfying to the alumni, students, and school.

How Successful Are Job Services?

Ask to see data on the success rates of the school's job placement services. The school should be able to provide you with information on job placement rates of recent graduating classes. Data usually include the length of time of the job search, the average salary obtained, the types of settings where graduates obtained employment, and the locations of the jobs obtained.

If the school does not have data or is vague in its response, ask what methods the school uses in evaluating the efficacy of its job placement efforts. If you still do not receive some level of information, think over your options of schools carefully.

Achievements of Alumni

The job placement data on recent graduating classes should give you a sense of how recent graduates do in the short run. It is also important to get a sense of how the school's graduates achieve in the long run. Can the school provide you with information on typical career paths of graduates in the school's various areas of concentration?

Can the school put you in contact with alumni practicing in the area of social work of your interest? A candid conversation with an alumnus may include questions such as his assessment of how well the program prepared him for the type of work he does. You may also want to find out how graduates of the school are perceived in the field. Are they thought of primarily as clinicians, administrators or policy specialists, or some combination? If he had to make a choice again about a graduate program, would he still attend the same school? Of course, take the answers as coming from someone who is clearly biased on behalf of the school. After all, it is unlikely the school will give you the name and phone number of a dissatisfied alumnus. Nevertheless, the conversation should be helpful to you.

Helpful Hints

Do...

- evaluate library facilities.
- check that state-of-the-art computer facilities are available. They are a most important part of your education because you will need those skills wherever you go in the future.
- look at the quality, proximity, and safety of housing.
- inquire about the availability of alternative bookstores. They can save you a great deal of money when compared with campus bookstores' often exorbitant prices.
- inquire about recreational opportunities in the area ("All work and no play...").
- check the availability of advising and job placement services.

Don't...

- overlook support facilities and services.
- make a final decision about a school without visiting it.
- overlook safety issues.
- think you won't get sick, or possibly suffer an accident, while a student. Check out the cost and quality of healthcare and insurance.
- overlook inquiring about alumni achievements and involvement. They can be valuable resources while you are a student, in your job search upon graduation, and beyond.

Part II

What Schools Look For In Applicants

What Schools Look For In Applicants

The mechanism by which schools of social work review applications varies. For purposes of discussion, the term "Admissions Committee" is used throughout this Guide *to refer to the group of people charged with the responsibility of reviewing applications. In some schools, administrators and faculty rotate serving on the admissions committee for a term of several academic years. As many as one third of the faculty may be on the committee at any point in time. In this model, the committee members may be asked to read applications and rate each applicant according to predetermined standards on a rater's form. A few schools include second-year master's students on the committee as actual readers of applications with rating responsibility at par with faculty members. Sometimes two separate raters review each application independently and the admissions director or another administrator makes the final decision based on the ratings of each applicant relative to the applicant pool. A variation on this model may be that the admissions director makes decisions for applicants who are either clearly not qualified or clearly qualified for admission and sends all other applicants to committee. Another model may be that the admissions director makes all admissions decisions, without the aid of a committee. Whatever model of review a school employs, most employ a dual lens in evaluating applicants.*

Most programs of social work attempt to answer two questions regarding each applicant. The first is, "Does the applicant show evidence of academic preparation and the ability to succeed in a graduate program?" Once that question has been answered affirmatively, the school asks, "How has the applicant tested his or her interest in the field of social service and what potential contributions can the applicant make to the profession?"

Part II will look more closely at these two areas and offer strategies you may employ to enhance your preparation for application to MSW programs. Additional suggestions are presented to help you succeed in those programs and beyond.

Chapter 7

Evidence of Academic Preparation

In general, schools of social work attempt to evaluate the applicant's academic preparation and potential for graduate study in several ways. One way is to look at the applicant's performance as reflected in the undergraduate grade point average (GPA). Beyond that, admissions committees use letters of reference from academic sources to obtain a picture of the candidate that may not emerge from the GPA. Some schools attempt to evaluate potential for graduate work by requiring applicants to submit scores from standardized tests such as the Graduate Record Examination (GRE) or the Miller Analogies Test (MAT), while other schools make tests optional. A few schools require personal interviews. The large number of applicants makes interviews for every applicant impractical. Most schools, therefore, invite only selected applicants for interviews.

Although not often considered as such by many applicants, the supplementary statement (referred to by various names including, among others, biographical statement or statement of purpose) also serves to gauge academic preparation, because it serves as a sample of the applicant's writing. The supplementary statement's importance cannot be overemphasized, both as a writing sample and as a vehicle to expound on the factors that contributed to an interest in the field, actual experiences, and educational and professional goals. General aspects of the supplementary statement are discussed in Chapter 10 of this book. Questions normally found in statement instructions, and how to best address them, are detailed in Chapter 11.

The Undergraduate Record

Let's look first at the undergraduate record. The degree to which schools are interested in a particular undergraduate major field of study varies. Most seek applicants with a broad and solid liberal arts background. A good way to ascertain your schools' position is to ask for figures on the percentages of different undergraduate majors among recently admitted applicants. At one major school, the "big three" undergraduate majors admitted each year are psychology, sociology, and social work. It is not uncommon, however, for over sixty percent of each incoming class to have undergraduate majors in such diverse fields as nursing, criminal justice, communication, and business.

The Undergraduate Major

Having majored in social work in college does not necessarily place an applicant in a position of advantage. It should be noted, however, that undergraduate social work majors may have an advantage in that their undergraduate curriculum includes a field work placement. This aspect will be discussed at greater length in Chapter 9.

The Undergraduate GPA

More crucial than the undergraduate major itself is the applicant's performance, whatever the area of concentration. In addition to evaluating the candidate's overall grade point average (GPA), many schools compute the applicant's post-sophomore GPA. Indeed, many schools place more weight on the post-sophomore GPA than on the overall GPA. It is thought that the last two years of college are a much better indicator of the candidate's academic ability and potential for graduate study.

Performance in the first two years of college is often affected by experimentation with different majors and by a period of adjustment to college. Many a college career has begun with well-intentioned efforts in a major that proves outside of a student's interests and abilities. The result can be mediocre to poor grades. By the same token, living away from home for the first time or readjusting to an academic environment after years in the work-a-day world can also result in less than optimal academic performance.

By the last two years of college, the reasoning goes, the candidate has negotiated the adjustment to college and has settled into a major field of study. In addition, course work in the last two years is more advanced and more comparable to graduate study. Many introductory college courses, although of prime importance in preparing students for later work, are not particularly challenging in the areas of verbal and written expression and critical thinking. Many examinations in introductory survey courses are objective and do not require the ability to synthesize, analyze, and present a coherent written essay response as is often the case in more advanced classes.

Therefore, it is generally presumed that work in the last two years of college requires the development of analytical and communication skills. Those skills are critical in graduate social work education and in professional practice.

This is not to say, however, that the first two years of college are disregarded. The overall GPA is also considered, but usually not to the degree of the post-sophomore GPA. I state this to caution readers who may be in the early part of their college careers and may be tempted to think they can afford to do less than their best now. A good foundation now will increase the chances of good performance later.

A second word of warning: As an admissions officer, I was often asked by genuinely bewildered applicants why they had been denied admission when their GPA in their major was high. More often than not, the answer was that their GPA outside their major was mediocre to poor. Although your performance in your major field of study is important, so is your performance elsewhere. Do not make the mistake of thinking that grades in some courses are "irrelevant" to your graduate school application.

Those readers who are attending, or attended, an undergraduate institution that emphasizes analytic and communication skills throughout its curriculum may take issue with my statement that the first two years of college are not generally thought of as particularly challenging in the areas of verbal expression and critical thinking. Be assured that admissions committees of most schools take into account the quality of the undergraduate institution the applicant attended. Those applicants who challenged themselves by attending undergraduate institutions with particularly rigorous programs generally will not be at a disadvantage if they have a slightly lower GPA than applicants who attended less demanding programs.

On the other hand, applicants will generally not be at a disadvantage regardless of the perceived quality of their undergraduate school. Admissions committees realize that an applicant's choice of undergraduate program is often influenced by financial or personal factors. The need to stay close to one's family as a source of financial support, for example, places geographic limits beyond the applicant's control. The real issue is how well the applicant performed.

Undergraduate Narrative Evaluations

There are a number of undergraduate institutions that have moved away from letter grading systems to narrative evaluations. If the college you attended subscribes to that type of evaluation, you will not have a GPA, because there will be no grades to compute.

The primary step you must take is to be a very early applicant. Inquire of the graduate schools what is the earliest possible date you can submit your application. I recommend this because very few people apply early. Therefore, assuming the school reviews applications on a rolling basis (as most do), there will be few applications to read early in the review cycle. The admissions committee will be able to take its time in reading your narrative evaluations.

If, on the other hand, you make application late in the year or, worse yet, on or near the final deadline, the committee will have many more applications to read. The chances of your application being given the time it requires will be very low.

Undergraduate Electives

I stated earlier that the particular major is not as important as the level of academic performance. Nevertheless, it is important to provide the graduate admissions committee with evidence of some "rhyme and reason" behind your course selection. The major and other course selections should support your proposed field of concentration for graduate study. For example, if you propose to focus on clinical social work, a foundation in undergraduate clinical psychology or clinical social work course sequences is advisable.

On the other hand, if you anticipate a focus on social administration or on broader policy aspects of social welfare in graduate school, your undergraduate record should indicate some preparation in the areas of macroeconomics, political systems, and related subjects. Master's programs seek students who have made a conscientious effort to inform themselves thoroughly before making a choice of graduate study.

Some schools require or strongly recommend a minimum of 60 semester hours in the liberal arts. Some add the stipulation that at least 30 of those hours be in the social and behavioral sciences. A good foundation in the humanities might include courses in English, languages, literature, fine arts, philosophy, and religious studies. Courses in the areas of the social and behavioral sciences might include American government, anthropology, behavioral disabilities, economics, geography, history, legal studies, ethnic studies, child development, and psychology.

Classes in Research and Statistics

Whatever your intended graduate focus, it is important to have preparation in the area of research and statistics. Most graduate schools of social work require, or at a minimum strongly recommend, an undergraduate course in research and statistics.

If you have been out of college for some time and you had courses in research and statistics, check with the graduate schools you are considering to see if (a) they have a requirement for research and statistics courses and (b), if they do, if there is a time limit for having taken the course. Some schools require that the course be taken within the five or seven years preceding matriculation to graduate school. The reasoning is two-fold: unless the person has been involved continuously in research, it is unlikely the concepts have been retained. In addition, the field of research and statistics evolves at such a rapid pace that many concepts become outdated, or at least altered, fairly quickly.

Many undergraduate programs in the social sciences offer a two-course sequence in research and statistics. Social science research courses are preferable to business-oriented courses. The quasi-experimental nature of social science research is much more applicable and relevant to graduate study in social work than the more pure research found in the natural sciences and business. In addition to a level of familiarity with research and statistics, many graduate schools of social work require at least one course in human biology.

A word of comfort is in order at this time. Many potential applicants to graduate programs in social work find the prospect of graduate level research and statistics somewhat intimidating. I count myself among that number, as I think back to my days in graduate school. Be assured that, although demanding and certainly not to be taken for granted, research and statistics classes at the master's level are not intended to make researchers out of students. (That's what doctoral programs are for.)

Rather, their intent is for master's level practitioners to acquire an understanding of research practice and methods, so they may be informed professionals capable of discerning between solid and not-so-solid data they will undoubtedly encounter in their careers.

Helpful Hints

Do...

- assume your grades in *every* undergraduate class are important.
- take steps to make your choice of undergraduate major and other course selections support your proposed field of concentration for graduate study.
- have a good mix of liberal arts, social and behavioral sciences, and humanities courses in your undergraduate record.

Don't...

- assume having an undergraduate major in social work is mandatory.
- assume grades in non-social work courses are irrelevant.
- neglect to take classes in research and statistics while an undergraduate.

Chapter 8

Potential for Graduate Work

Besides convincing admissions committees that you are academically prepared for graduate work, you must show them that you have the potential to succeed in graduate school and in the social work profession. This chapter will address some of the ways admissions committees assess this potential—through academic letters of reference, test scores, and interviews.

Academic Letters of Reference

In this chapter, I will comment only on academic references and save remarks on professional references for the chapter on exposure to the profession of social work. A good rule of thumb on the types of references is to have half the letters submitted from academic sources and the other half from professional sources. This recommendation is in keeping with the general rule that committees on admission are looking at your application through the dual lenses of academic preparation/potential and exposure and suitability for the profession of social work.

Number of Letters

All graduate schools of social work require applicants for admission to submit letters of reference. The number of letters required varies by school, ranging from three to six. Some give applicants some latitude in the number of letters. For example, a school might request a minimum of four and a maximum of six letters of reference.

It is very important that you keep track of the specific requirements of the various schools to which you make application. An "MSW Application Tracking Sheet" is provided in Appendix E of this book to assist you. One school I am familiar with disqualifies a number of applicants every year because of incomplete applications. It is the only school in its region to request a minimum of four letters of reference, whereas all the other area schools require only three letters. Invariably, a number of applicants fail to send in a fourth letter and find themselves with incomplete applications. It may seem too obvious a point to mention, yet it is worth recommending you keep careful track of the timely submission of all the required materials to each school.

If a school gives you an option as to the number of letters to submit (i.e., a minimum of four letters and a maximum of six), don't assume you will be at a disadvantage if you submit fewer letters than the maximum allowed. If the school needed or wanted the maximum number, it would have said so; take it at its word. In general, it is better to be very judicious about the types of references and their sources. I've seen applicants who would have been much better off with one less reference that offered vague or unkind comments.

Sources of the Letters

Academic references are more relevant if they come from professors in social work classes or related fields such as psychology or sociology. Letters from professors who taught you research and statistics are highly recommended. In addition, letters from professors who have a good knowledge of your analytical and writing abilities are useful.

Without disputing the value of other classes to a comprehensive education, letters from professors of art, theater, and other fields that are less related to social work are not your best choices, unless you majored in one of those fields. Given that most MSW faculty, who comprise admissions committees, may not be familiar with those fields, you may have to do some educating of admissions committees in your biographical statement about the academic demands of your undergraduate major.

Request letters from professors who have a good grasp of your academic abilities through multiple classes. It is not a good idea to request letters from professors that you only had for one class, perhaps an introductory class, several semesters ago. The professor may not remember much about you but may be too embarrassed to admit it. The result will be a reference that is vague, lacking in enthusiasm, and fails to provide any meaningful insight to the admissions committee.

I have been asked many times if references from alumni of the graduate school to which you are applying are preferable to nonalumni. The answer is they may or may not be. On the surface, it would seem that alumni are a good source, because they can comment from firsthand knowledge of the school on their perception of your suitability for the program, as well as your potential for success in the program. On the other hand, how their comments are received by the school will depend on how the school views the particular alumnus/a. His or her opinions may be highly valued or they may not hold much meaning. Unfortunately, in most instances you will not be in a position to know the last factor. My recommendation is not to let whether or not a person is an alumna be the primary reason for selecting her as a reference.

Timing Your Request

It is very important, and simple common courtesy, to allow your references plenty of time to write the letters. Composing a good reference requires time to carefully consider your strengths and potential. Many applicants do not allow enough time—and place themselves, and their sources, in the uncomfortable position of last-minute reminders by phone and other means. The results are letters that are never what they could have been.

Take into account the source's schedule and other responsibilities. For example, asking a professor to produce a letter of reference in one week's time during midterms or finals is highly unreasonable. Asking him to take time from holidays is also not a good idea. In general, allow a good four weeks or more during periods that are not unusually hectic.

Under the right circumstances, most professors consider it a pleasure and a privilege to write letters of reference. After all, they were in your shoes at some point in the past. Despite your best efforts at asking at the right time and allowing plenty of time, there will be sources who do not respond promptly. In those circumstances, delicacy and tact are your best allies.

Keeping Track of Letters

In an effort to cut back on administrative expenses, many graduate schools of social work are moving toward an "applicant-managed" application. What that means is that the applicant collects all the application materials and submits them together to the school. If this is the case, your reference sources will be giving you their completed references. This is usually done in a sealed envelope, sometimes supplied by the school in the application packet, that is signed across the seal by the author of the reference.

It is important to make it very clear to your reference sources what they are to do with the completed reference. Given that the applicant-managed model of application is fairly recent, many of the professors in the field today may not be familiar with it. Therefore, they may believe that they need to mail their completed references directly to the school.

If they do that, it may cause some confusion for the school and more work for you. If it does happen, contact the school immediately to explain the situation and verify that the letter was received and that it will be held until you send in the rest of your application. Write down the name of the person you speak with, and when you submit your application, include a letter referencing the conversation and the name of the person with whom you spoke.

One possible way to avoid confusion is to give your sources stamped self-addressed envelopes they may use to return the reference to you. If the schools you are applying to require the sources to send the letters directly to the school, it is also a good idea for you to provide a stamped, addressed envelope.

If You Can't Locate Professors

If it has been several years since you graduated from college, it may be difficult to impossible for you to locate your former professors. If you do find them—depending on how much time has elapsed—they may not remember much about you. Do your best to locate at least one of your professors. When you do, tactfully remind her of your experiences in her class. She may be flattered that you remember her and, consequently, be hesitant to mention she does not remember you. She will appreciate any hints you offer. If you are compulsive enough to have kept your college papers, offering to send a copy of a paper you wrote for one of her classes would be most useful.

Don't despair if you are unable to contact any former professors because it has been a long time since you left college. Admissions committees understand your predicament. I suggest a brief explanatory footnote in the place on the application where you list your reference sources. Briefly bring to the committee's attention that you were unable to locate former professors because of the passage of time. If it has only been two or three years or less since you finished college, however, the committee may not be as understanding.

If you are unable to provide academic references, you can still provide what I call "pseudo-academic" references. Current or former employers in settings that require academic skills will serve this purpose. Positions that require the ability to analyze complex problems, formulate solutions, and use exceptional verbal and written communication skills are good options.

Letters From Relatives

I'll make one final note on letters of reference. Letters from relatives should not be used. Period. Although not all schools make it explicit that letters from relatives are not allowed, I highly advise against their use. Even if the relative is in a professional position to comment knowledgeably on the applicant's academic and professional abilities, the fact that the opinions are being rendered by a relative casts a shadow of doubt.

I have seen marvelous letters of reference from relatives that are simply dismissed by the committee. In addition, the committee may wonder if the person is of such limited ability and academic or professional exposure that he cannot locate other people who can offer references.

Standardized Test Scores

Some graduate schools of social work require applicants to submit scores from the Graduate Record Examination (GRE) or the Miller Analogies Test (MAT). Other schools give applicants the option of submitting scores. Still other schools do not require scores for admission, but either require them or strongly recommend them for scholarship applicants. Contact the schools you are interested in to learn their specific requirements.

In those cases in which applicants have a choice about GRE or MAT scores, applicants who are confident that their undergraduate record reflects their abilities often opt not to submit scores. On the other hand, applicants whose undergraduate records were affected by personal circumstances often opt to submit scores as a way to strengthen their applications. The wrong decision can hurt any applicant regardless of his GPA. If your GPA is high, do not submit scores unless they are also high. If your GPA is low but so are your GRE or MAT scores, don't submit scores; there is no need to add to the evidence against you.

If you find you need to submit standardized test scores, do not take the task lightly. I strongly recommend you explore preparatory courses or, at the very least, invest in a self-guided preparatory manual. I feel strongly about this subject, because I have seen well-qualified candidates "shoot themselves in the foot" with poor scores. Poor scores on the GRE or MAT can cast doubt on even the best of college grades. Allow yourself plenty of rest the night before the exam and approach it calmly and methodically.

When to Request Scores

Do not request that your scores be sent to any graduate school before you know how well you scored. It will cost more to order reports later, but it will be well worth the expense. By so doing, you will have the opportunity to make informed decisions on whether or not to submit scores to those schools that make scores optional. If your GPA is high, don't risk hurting your chances of admission with low GRE or MAT scores if you can help it. I have, on occasion, seen instances when applicants with very high GPAs were denied admission because they made the tactical error of submitting low scores to schools where scores were optional.

To make a better decision on whether or not to submit GRE or MAT scores, inquire what the range, mean, median, and mode were for the most recent admissions cycle at the schools that interest you. For the more competitive, nationally-ranked schools, if your GRE scores average below 650 on the test sections and your GPA is in the vicinity of 3.2 or above on a 4.0 scale, it is probably best not to submit scores if you have the option.

Timing of the Test

When you take the test is also important. I suggest taking it late in your third year of college or early in your fourth year. By so doing, you have time to make the critical decisions of whether or not to use the scores or attempt to retake the test.

Taking the test early will also insure you meet the schools' application deadlines. Many an otherwise qualified applicant has been disqualified because she took the test late and scores did not reach graduate schools by their deadlines.

Interviews

The large number of applicants has made it impractical at most schools to make a personal interview a required part of the admissions process. Some schools reserve the right to invite selected applicants for interviews. Generally, the applicants invited to interview are few and usually are invited because they may present a unique profile. For example, it may be someone who appears an excellent candidate in all aspects but one. Grades might be excellent but the quality of experiences questionable, or the applicant might be a "career-changer" who the admissions committee wants to meet to get a better sense of the reasons for the change. Check with the schools of your choice on their interview policies.

Informal Interviews

Having said that, let me add that in actuality, interviews take place regularly. Even though a school may not grant formal interviews, applicants who make a visit to campus and meet with school officials can use the opportunity as a sort of interview. During my time in admissions, I often met with prospective applicants I found particularly impressive. In such instances, I would write a memorandum to the admissions committee highlighting my impressions. Please note that I would not write a memorandum for every prospect that visited—only for those who projected qualities that I felt were not reflected in the written application materials.

If you will be visiting a school, I suggest preparing thoroughly and formulating well thought-out questions. The questions for your school visit in Appendix F provide a starting point. In addition, review the interests and publications of the faculty (generally found in the school's catalog) and identify those with interests similar to your own. Ask if it would be possible to meet with the faculty members you identify. If it is possible to meet with faculty, read some of their work and be prepared to discuss it intelligently. Be aware that the faculty member(s) may not be available. Normally, meetings with specific faculty members are reserved for applicants to doctoral programs. If you do get the opportunity, take full advantage of it at the levels of (a) learning more about the school and (b) possibly increasing your chances of admission.

One particular case comes to mind that illustrates the benefits of this strategy. An applicant visited the school and met with a faculty member. The faculty person was so impressed with the applicant's grasp of the field and his future goals that the faculty person wrote a memorandum to the admissions committee on the applicant's behalf. The applicant was offered admission, despite a marginal GPA. It is unlikely he would have been admitted without the added factor of the memorandum from the faculty member. The applicant went on to excel in the program and became a respected student leader among his peers.

Should you be offered and accept admission, there is another possible advantage of having met with a faculty member. Often, particularly at schools with very prolific researchers, the faculty member you meet with may be working on a research project that employs students. You will have a distinct advantage over other prospective student employees. Often, student positions are never openly listed because researchers fill them from students they know. Aside from providing you with a nice source of income while you are a student, a job in research will round out your résumé a good deal better than a job, say, stacking books in the library.

Helpful Hints

Do...

- strive for a balance in reference letters by having half of the letters submitted be from academic sources and the other half from professional sources.
- keep careful track of the timely submission of all the required materials, including letters of reference, to each school.
- be very judicious about the types of references and their sources.
- if they are needed, take standardized tests early enough to review scores before deciding whether or not to submit them to schools.
- treat any contact with any school representative as an interview. Make no mistake about it, it is.

Don't...

- ask for references at the last minute. Be respectful of the person you are asking.
- be too concerned if, as someone who attended college many years ago, you cannot locate professors to seek references.
- submit letters of reference from relatives.
- submit standardized test scores until you know what they are.

Chapter 9

Exposure to the Profession

The term "graduate school" is used throughout this book, and is generally widely used, in reference to schools of social work. In reality, schools of social work are not "graduate schools" in the traditional academic sense. Instead, they belong more in the classification of professional schools. Much as schools of business train for professional practice in the world of business, schools of law train for the professional practice of law, and schools of medicine train for the professional practice of medicine, schools of social work provide training for the professional practice of social work. Of necessity, the training is not purely academic. Schools of social work are not preparing individuals for purely academic endeavors. They are training professionals for delicate practice with living human beings, and these professionals bring backgrounds and needs as varied as the clients themselves.

Therefore, it is important, and indeed inescapable, that the admissions process include an evaluation of factors much broader than simply academic merits. The demonstrated ability to perform academically is crucial but it is only a beginning point. The ability to integrate the theoretical knowledge base into compassionate and effective practice is the measure of the social work professional. Beyond scholarly ability, the applicant must show evidence of a sensitivity to human needs and the ability to interact with diverse groups of people across a span of system levels.

Without this added dimension, the highly academically qualified applicant falls short. The weight given to experiential factors is normally the same as that given to academic factors in admission decisions at most MSW programs. When asked in a 1999 survey by *The New Social Worker* magazine what advice they would give potential applicants, one of the most frequent responses of recent graduates and current students at MSW programs was to obtain plenty of field experience. They cited that experience is helpful at multiple levels. Schools look for evidence of firsthand knowledge of the field, the experience helps students integrate class material, and experiences help clarify if social work is indeed the profession they prefer.

The settings where aspiring MSW applicants can gain experience are as varied as the options in the field of social work itself. Before discussing the settings themselves, it will be useful to identify the general principles valuable for social work practice that you should seek to be exposed to before applying to schools of social work. I hope that an understanding of the principles will allow you to identify settings I may not mention. Nevertheless, later in this chapter I will offer specifics on potential settings, how each may relate to your particular goals, and suggestions for locating them.

The Basic Principles of Social Work

Historically, the profession of social work has concerned itself with serving those who would not otherwise be served. In its infancy at the turn of the century, social work was concerned with universal social security, child labor, and similar issues affecting the disenfranchised and powerless. To be sure, the passage of time has brought increased sophistication in terms of the theoretical foundations and methods utilized, but the basic mission remains the same: to help individuals improve their social functioning and status.

In its very name, the profession recognizes the need to view the individual in his social context. Social workers seek to understand the interplay of various systemic factors affecting individuals. For example, the Statement of Purpose of the School of Social Service Administration of the University of Chicago states, in part, "Individual distress occurs in a social context involving the interaction of biological, psychological, familial, economic, and cultural factors."

Issues Addressed by Social Work

The issues addressed by the many types of social work being practiced today are as broad and varied as our society. Many challenges faced by social workers lie in the areas of child welfare, housing and homelessness, poverty, violence, psychiatric disorders, developmental disabilities, physical disabilities, substance abuse, sexuality, legal, and a host of other issues.

Keep in mind that the real world is never as neatly divided as categories in any book would lead you to believe. In the real world, categories often overlap and distinctions are easily blurred. So is the case in the real world of professional social work practice. For the purpose of our discussion, I will focus on the major areas of child welfare services, housing and homelessness, and psychiatric and substance abuse treatment. The issues of poverty, violence, and legal system involvement cut across all categories to one extent or another.

Child Welfare

The category of child welfare services, for instance, can encompass a wide variety of job functions and settings. As with all categories, the range of functions can be classified virtually anywhere along the continuum from purely direct service to purely administrative or policy oriented. Whatever their specific function, social workers in the field of social welfare are primarily concerned with the well-being of children and adolescents.

Clinical positions in child welfare include hospital social workers focusing on maternal and child health, case managers for women and children infected and affected by the HIV virus, therapists for wards of the state with emotional and behavior problems, therapists in Employee Assistance Programs specializing in child and family issues, family crisis intervention counselors, school social workers, counselors in family preservation programs, caseworkers in state departments for family and children services, therapists for child physical and sexual abuse offenders, child abuse investigators, protective services workers, foster home developers, and domestic violence counselors.

Settings for child welfare clinical practice include community mental health centers; domestic violence shelters; hospitals/clinics; private clinical practice; state departments of child and family services; private companies and corporations; Head Start programs; psychiatric centers; non-profit organizations; county, state, and other governmental agencies; residential treatment centers; churches; community crisis centers; court systems; public schools; foster care agencies; and public health programs.

Administrative and policy positions and settings in child welfare include administrators of community mental health centers; strategic planners on child welfare services at the local, state, or federal levels of government; policy analysts for grassroots agencies reviewing systemic community child welfare problems and gathering data for lobbying efforts; directors of child welfare initiatives at foundations allocating funds to create and sustain comprehensive, integrated, community-based service systems for children, youth, and their families; grant and proposal writers consulting with community organizations; community education coordinators in community programs providing programs on sexual abuse prevention, truancy prevention, gang prevention, and similar topics; trainers and facilitators for public child welfare workers; investigators/researchers in college or university-based centers for children studies; coordinators of adoption services in public or private agencies; and administrators of organizations for purposes of lobbying on children's issues.

Housing and Homelessness

Clinical positions and settings in the area of housing and homelessness include workers at homeless shelters, workers at shelters for victims of domestic violence, examiner and licenser of emergency and long-term foster homes, workers at senior housing centers, and social workers at extended care facilities.

Administrative and policy positions and settings in the field of housing and homelessness include administrators for housing and economic development councils, foundation grant officers specializing in housing initiatives, community reinvestment specialists at financial institutions, administrators at shelters for the homeless, and administrators at shelters for victims of domestic violence.

Psychiatric and Substance Abuse Treatment

For well over the past thirty years, the vast majority of mental health services in the United States have been delivered by social workers. Only in the recent past have states come to recognize social workers as independent practitioners through legislation that makes provisions for licensure, certification, or registration of social workers. As of 1993, all states and the District of Columbia had laws in those regards.

Social workers practice as clinical therapists, family therapists, clinical supervisors, mental health workers and therapists, substance abuse counselors, psychiatric social workers, and in many other related positions. The settings include community mental health centers, hospitals and clinics, private clinical practice, child and family service agencies, day treatment programs, psychiatric centers, domestic violence centers, councils on alcoholism, and many other clinical settings. By the same token, social workers can be found in administrative and policy-making positions in all clinical settings.

Cross-Over Issues

Because of the fundamental nature of the social work profession and the population it is pledged to serve, most social workers are in some way dealing with issues of poverty, violence, and the legal system. For example, clinical social workers providing therapeutic services in community mental health centers have many clients with multiple concerns, including poverty, violence, and substance abuse across system levels. Some clinical positions more directly related to issues of poverty include employment services coordinators at private and public agencies, vocational counselors, human rights spokespersons, and community organizers in poverty-stricken communities.

Some administrative and policy positions and settings more closely related to issues of poverty include administrators of public housing projects, administrators of economic development entities in the community or at foundations, and planners for city departments of planning and development. Workers at correctional institutions also deal more directly with issues of violence as do workers in courts, at shelters for victims of domestic violence, in state agencies for the prevention of child and adult abuse, community crisis intervention centers, and hospitals.

Locating A Site for Gaining Exposure to Social Service

It is hoped the above overview of areas of practice and settings of social workers will provide you with a starting point. Carefully evaluate where your interests may best be served. If you are more attracted to direct work with individuals, groups, and families, seek a clinical site. If, on the other hand, you find the broader aspects of program planning, fund raising, and program evaluation intriguing, seek an administrative or policy setting.

It is important that you recognize that if your level of experience is minimal, the level of autonomy and direct involvement you will be allowed will be equally minimal, regardless of the setting. Nevertheless, firsthand exposure, even if only at the level of observer, will be beneficial to your growth and in demonstrating to social work schools your commitment to the field.

Once you've tentatively identified your potential settings of interest, there are some excellent sources for beginning the search. Your local United Way office will probably have information on agencies that seek volunteers. In fact, most chapters of United Way publish a listing of volunteer opportunities. They are in an excellent position to know, because many community agencies receive United Way funding to one extent or another. You can call the United Way of America at 703-836-7100 or toll-free at 800-411-8929 to get the telephone number of your state or local United Way chapter.

Another good source is your college or university's career and placement office. Agencies and organizations that seek volunteers realize that college students make excellent volunteers because of their educational levels and sincere enthusiasm. Agencies are wise to cultivate good relations with their community's educational institutions.

If your college or university has a community relations office, so much the better. Many educational institutions have come to recognize how important it is to be thought of as a good neighbor and devote considerable resources to that goal. A good community relations office will have listings of volunteer opportunities in the community and may even offer stipends to students who participate in selected projects.

Another good source is your state chapter of the National Association of Social Workers (NASW). NASW has chapters in all fifty states, as well as New York City; Metro Washington, DC; Puerto Rico; the Virgin Islands; and an International chapter. You may reach the national office of NASW toll-free at 1-800-638-8799 to learn how to contact your state or local NASW chapter.

A word about NASW is appropriate here. NASW is the national organization for social workers in this country. It has been instrumental in achieving tremendous progress in the provision of social services through legislation at the national, state, and local levels. NASW was instrumental in achieving certification or licensure of social workers in every state.

I highly recommend you explore the benefits of NASW membership. Rates are extremely reasonable for students. As of October 1999, regular membership dues are $160/year; the student rate is $40/year. Those who join NASW as students also qualify for a reduced transitional rate for a period of time after graduation. I know of no better way to stay abreast of developments in the field of social work than through membership in NASW. It should be noted, however, that you must be a current student in a Council on Social Work Education accredited social work degree program or a program eligible for candidacy to be eligible for student membership in NASW. Other categories of membership require an accredited degree, other than associate membership, which requires that you be employed in a social work capacity and have at least a bachelor's degree in a field other than social work. I should mention that I have been an active member of NASW for many years, and my recommendation of NASW is purely voluntary.

Selecting The Site

Once you've identified several possible sites that accept volunteers, it will be time to carefully assess which will be most beneficial for you. One factor to consider is the reputation of the agency or institution. If it is a national organization, it will be known to many schools of social work to which you make application for admission. If it is a local or regional organization, it may only be known to schools within your region.

This is not to say that small local agencies will not be excellent settings. One way to overcome the factor of the agency not being known to schools when you apply is to ask the person from the agency who writes you a reference to include a brief statement of the agency's mission and services.

You may also want to inquire of the local Better Business Bureau (BBB) about any consumer complaints the Bureau has received about the agency. Unfortunately, there are some agencies that undergo periods of extreme unethical practices under a bad administration. I know of at least one agency that had a former top level officer placed in a witness protection program in exchange for testifying to corrupt practices. The same agency has recovered nicely over the years and currently has an excellent reputation thanks to new leadership. Having served as a volunteer or intern in an agency during questionable times may not be good for you.

It does not hurt to look ahead. Your graduation from an MSW program may seem far away at this time, but it will be here before you know it. Therefore, consider if the agency is large enough to be an employment possibility for you in the future. I know of several colleagues who have risen through the ranks at agencies where they once volunteered as college students.

What Will You Be Doing?

Of more immediate concern, of course, is the question of what your duties will be as a volunteer. Be candid with the agency about your future educational plans in social work. Whereas you should be realistic about the things you are capable of doing at this time, you should also expect to be in a position to at least be exposed to learning experiences.

A position that keeps you filing membership records in a back room, for instance, will do little for your professional growth. On the other hand, opportunities to assist staff in community education programs on issues such as parenting or child abuse prevention, even if initially only in arranging the classroom, registering participants, and observing the program, will be very beneficial.

Seek Learning Opportunities

Most agencies provide continuing education for their staff as part of their licensing and funding source requirements. Some agencies provide workshops either in-house or send their employees to outside seminars and conferences. Ask if as a volunteer or intern you will be afforded the same opportunities. They can greatly contribute to your knowledge of the field and your professional growth. In addition, being able to document in your MSW applications for admission that you have participated in social work-related continuing education will be a big plus.

Who Will Supervise You?

Another very important aspect to consider is the background of the person you will be working for. Although not a must, it would be very helpful to work for a person with a background in social work or in a related field, preferably at the master's level. Working with a social worker will familiarize you with the perspective that guides our profession.

Down the road, a letter of reference from the supervisor of your volunteer experience as you apply to master's programs will serve you well. Letters from social work professionals have added credibility, because they can comment on the person's suitability for a graduate social work education and the profession from the perspective of one who has experienced it.

Your Conduct On Site

Once you select a volunteer site and are on the job, be sure to approach all work with the agency with the same high level of dedication and diligence as if it were a full-time paid position. The profession of social work is small and one's reputation is one's calling card. Most social workers in a given region, and in some cases across regions or even nationally, come to meet each other at seminars, workshops, conferences or other events. Many serve on boards of directors of several agencies or even at some graduate programs of social work. Begin cultivating a sound reputation now and it will serve you well later.

Helpful Hints

Do...

- keep in mind that weight given to experiential factors is normally the same as that given to academic factors in admission decisions at most MSW programs.
- seek experiences in social work settings that will contribute to your development.
- attempt in your volunteer experiences to work for people with a background in social work or in a related field, preferably at the master's level.

Don't...

- fail to approach all volunteer work with the same high level of dedication and diligence as if it were a full-time paid position.
- forget to request a letter of reference from your supervisor and other professionals (especially social workers) familiar with your work in volunteer settings.

Chapter 10

The Biographical Statement: An Overview

All graduate schools of social work request that applicants submit a biographical statement. The essay may also be referred to as a supplementary statement, admissions essay, and by other similar titles. Whatever each institution chooses to call it, its purpose is the same. It is intended as a vehicle for the admissions committee to learn more about the applicant than mere grades on a transcript, standardized test scores, or letters of reference can convey. It is your opportunity to give the school a broader perspective of your background, experiences, and educational as well as professional goals. This chapter is intended to give you an overview of the biographical statement, while Chapter 11 provides more specifics on the typical questions found on instructions for biographical statements and how to formulate your responses.

How To Approach Writing Your Statement

I recommend that you perform a thorough self-assessment before writing your statement. Make a list of all jobs, volunteer positions, and internships you have ever held. In short, take an inventory of any experiences that somehow contributed to your interest in social work. Review Chapter 9 of this *Guide,* which discusses social work settings. Don't neglect to also list classes that you may have taken that contributed to the development of your interests. For some people, even an individual field trip taken as part of a class may have been significant. In Appendix G, you will find a worksheet that will help you organize your efforts in writing the biographical statement.

Chances are you've had some experiences in settings that you may not have previously considered related to social work. I've often met with students who tell me of jobs in research, legal offices, and other settings and then proceed to state they have no social work experience. They are surprised when I mention that certain types of research are very beneficial to aspiring social workers.

Even if the research was not directly related to social welfare issues, the exposure to the act of research is very useful. The aim of social research courses in MSW programs is to make students aware of the essentials of good research and the benefits of good research to an informed professional practice. Applicants seem equally surprised that an experience in a legal aid agency can serve as valuable exposure to clients who are at a crisis point in their lives and very much in need of assistance coping with many social systems around them.

Once you've made as comprehensive a list as possible, identify the skills you developed as a result of each particular experience. Chapter 9 discusses social work skills and may help you in this process. Keep in mind that the most important aspect in the experience is not necessarily the setting itself.

The most important elements are the skills you develop that are transferable to other settings. For example, the skills developed in interviewing clients are transferable to many other settings. People who seek services at a legal aid agency typically are experiencing financial difficulties, either of a temporary or chronic nature. They are also at a point in their lives when they are experiencing a life event of considerable stress, such as a divorce, eviction, or other event. They require an interviewer who can ease their anxiety and be empathic enough to allow them to express their needs at their own pace. Those skills are transferable to virtually any crisis setting.

A review of your experiences will be helpful not only in making an inventory of the skills you may have begun to develop, but also in identifying the areas of social work where you may want to go in the future. That awareness can help you immensely in determining which of the programs you are considering can best train you to achieve your goals.

By this point, you should be in an excellent position to make a strong case in your statement about why your experiences and goals are a good fit with the particular school's programs. For example, if your experiences have been in a pediatric hospital setting, you have probably begun to develop skills in the areas of assessing the impact of the onset of childhood illness on the family system. A careful evaluation of those skills can serve as a good foundation for assessing a school's maternal and child health program. In turn, the process can move to making a solid case for the suitability of the program to your educational and professional objectives.

It is difficult to overstate the importance of presenting a thoughtful and deliberate case of your reasons for wanting to be a social worker and for wanting to attend the particular program in your biographical statement. All other aspects of two applicants competing for a place in the class being equal, the person with the better biographical statement will win out. In the schools with more competitive admissions, most applicants have excellent undergraduate records and stellar references. What often separates them is the biographical statement. It often weighs as much or more than the undergraduate record and the references combined.

How Schools View Your Statement

Admissions committees view the biographical statement at a number of levels. At one level, the statement offers committees an understanding of how the applicant developed his interests in social work, and how he has tested his interests through employment, internships, and volunteer or personal experiences. By so doing, the statement gives the committee a sense of the degree to which the applicant's decision to pursue a career in social service is grounded in a solid and realistic view of the profession. Statements that do not accomplish this are generally of the "I've-always-been-a-people-person-and-I-want-to-work-with-people" type.

The statement also gives the committee a good understanding of the reasons behind the applicant's desire to pursue training for practice in a particular aspect of the profession. This is most important because admissions committees attempt to assess not only the applicant's suitability for the program, but also the program's suitability for meeting the person's educational and professional objectives.

At another level, the schools view the biographical statement as a sample of the applicant's writing. The ability to express oneself clearly and succinctly in written form is essential to success in a graduate program of social work. Most of the work graduate students of social work do consists of papers and essays and only a few objective tests. Furthermore, schools of social work believe that good writers are good thinkers. The ability to analyze problems and formulate sound and realistic solutions is central to being a social work student and professional.

At still another level, admissions committees view the biographical statement as a measure of how well the applicant follows instructions. You will serve yourself well by carefully following application instructions as they pertain to the biographical statement's format, areas of content, and length. It is not inaccurate to say that every word in every sentence of the instructions on any school's application was the subject of much thought and debate in admissions committee meetings. Committees expect applicants to be equally thorough and thoughtful in following those instructions. An applicant who neglects to do so is projecting an image of a sloppy and careless student graduate schools would rather do without.

The Cardinal Sins of Statement Writing

I strongly advise against using the same statement for the various schools to which you are making application. To be sure, you definitely should apply to more than one school. You should, however, write individual statements that conform to each school's requirements. It is tempting, in our age of computers and word processors, to simply alter a few items (such as the name of the school) and submit the same statement to all schools.

Each school has unique characteristics and programs. Tailor each school's statement to how your development and goals fit with each particular school's programmatic focus. Admission committees are quick to spot statements that speak eloquently about wanting to pursue a particular specialty that is not available in the school.

The most extreme case I've seen of the "mass production" of a statement was the case of an applicant who applied to school "A" and made a reasonable case why "A" was the best school for his goals, only to state in his closing remarks that he had always had the goal of attending school "B." He clearly made the mistake of not changing the name of the school uniformly as he printed the different versions of the same statement.

Another practice to avoid is over-focusing on personal psychological issues and treatment. Please refer to Chapter 11 of this book for specific recommendations on the judicious inclusion of information on personal psychological treatment. I recommend careful thought about mentioning past treatment for two reasons.

The first reason is that the committee may interpret excessive self-revelation as an indicator that you are seeking to enter the profession as a means to continue working on your personal issues. Unfortunately, many practicing professionals do a great disservice to their clients by failing to distinguish their own issues from those of the clients they treat. For the same reason, I discourage letters of reference from personal therapists.

The second reason that I discourage a great deal of self-revelation in the statement is that once your statement is in your file, it remains there through your time at the school and beyond. Most schools allow professors and even field instructors access to student files. A good rule of thumb is to not write anything in your statement you would not want professors, administrators, and field instructors to know.

A Final General Word About Your Statement

In short, the writing of the biographical statement is not to be taken lightly. If you have an outstanding undergraduate record and vainly (and foolishly!) believe no graduate school can afford to pass you up, think again. I have seen applicants to MSW programs who have multiple graduate degrees in related fields from the nation's finest institutions be denied admission. More often than not, they are denied because they took admission for granted and did a last-minute, careless job in composing their biographical statements.

In *The New Social Worker* magazine's 1999 survey of current MSW students and recent MSW graduates, many responded that the most stressful part of the MSW application process was composing the personal statement. When compared with papers you probably wrote as an undergraduate, the personal statement will appear deceptively simple. After all, most schools request only between three and five typewritten pages. The amount of introspection, exploration of future expectations and goals, and the need to match those to the particular program should not be taken lightly. Give yourself plenty of time to compose your statement thoughtfully and to have it critiqued for content and grammar.

Helpful Hints

Do...

- make a thorough self-assessment before writing your statement. Make a list of all jobs, volunteer positions, and internships you have ever held. In short, take an inventory of any experiences that somehow contributed to your interest in social work.
- identify the skills, and their application to social work, you developed as a result of each particular experience.
- make a strong case in your statement about why your experiences and goals are a good fit with the particular school's programs.
- remember that schools view the biographical statement as a sample of the applicant's writing. The ability to express oneself clearly and succinctly in written form is essential to success in a graduate program of social work.
- keep in mind that admissions committees view the biographical statement as a measure of how well the applicant follows instructions.
- remember that the writing of the biographical statement is not to be taken lightly, regardless of how marvelous your undergraduate record may be.

Don't...

- ignore experiences in settings that you may not have previously considered as social work-related.

(continued on next page)

(continued from previous page)

- underestimate the importance of presenting a thoughtful and deliberate case of your reasons for wanting to be a social worker and for attending the particular program in your biographical statement.

- write a statement that simply says, "I've-always-been-a-people-person-and-I-want-to-work-with-people."

- use identical statements for the various schools to which you are making application.

- over-focus in your statement on personal psychological issues and treatment.

Chapter 11

The Biographical Statement: The "Questions Behind the Questions"

Now that you have a general idea of the purposes of the biographical statement and how to approach it, let's turn our focus to the specifics of this aspect of your application.

Length, Content, and Format

Instructions provided by most, but not all, schools usually state a range for the length of the statement. In general, the length requested is from two to four typewritten, double-spaced pages. If a school you are considering does not specify length, it is a good idea to stay within the 2-4 page range. Whether a school provides limits or not, the length of the essay is a measure of the applicant's ability to be concise, yet thorough.

Most, but again, not all, schools provide a list of questions for the candidate to answer in the statement. A list of typical questions, and how to approach them, follows later in this chapter. If a school to which you are making application does not specify questions, it would be a good idea to follow the general questions listed in this chapter.

The format (i.e., the organization) is generally not specified in the instructions. The reason is that schools want to give applicants latitude in determining how to present their essays. The applicant's selection is, if you will, a gauge of their writing ability. Most applicants choose to write the statement as a narrative listing of their responses to the questions. Other applicants choose different and varied approaches. Whichever approach you select, it will be important that you address all of the points requested in the application instructions. It will be equally important to have a suitable introduction and conclusion.

Introducing Your Statement

How you choose to introduce your essay is very important. Some applicants begin the statement rather suddenly with details about their undergraduate concentration and how they came to be involved in social work. Although this approach may be factual and even substantive, it is much more advisable to begin with a well thought-out introduction (i.e., telling the reader what is ahead). This may seem somewhat unnecessary, because the readers on the admissions committee know full well what is ahead. After all, every applicant is given the same instructions. Other applicants choose to begin with a clever introduction, such as a quote or situation vignette from their lives or work experiences. There is a danger in attempting to be too clever. I suggest a more traditional, solid approach. Whichever way you select, a good beginning is crucial at several levels. One is that, in addition to content, the admissions committee looks for evidence of writing ability. At another level, a good beginning that engages the reader's attention is important to help your statement stand out among the many the committee reviews.

For example, you may choose to begin with a general introduction as follows:

Although my undergraduate concentration was in Juvenile Justice, I decided to explore the social work field beginning in my junior year. An internship that was to result in a job offer upon graduation served as a foundation to many later experiences professionally and as a volunteer in civic and other organizations.

By having an introduction that foreshadows what is ahead, you are arousing the interest of the reader to learn how your internship sparked your interest and what happened thereafter.

Typical Statement Questions

All schools provide applicants with some form of instructions for the personal or biographical statement. Most actually list a number of questions that should be addressed. Some, however, do not provide questions and limit the instructions to length of the statement and give the applicant a wide latitude as to what to include in the statement. Although the questions and their specific wording vary from school to school, in general, they fall into several categories. The categories are:

- Describe your social work experiences and why you have selected social work
- Describe your educational goals and expectations
- Describe your short- and long-term professional goals
- Provide evidence of your capacity for graduate work
- Describe why you seek a graduate social work education at this point in your career

Question 1: Describe Your Social Work Experiences and Why You Have Selected Social Work

This portion of your essay should not read like a résumé in narrative form. Given that most applications already have a section on your volunteer, internship, and paid experiences, you do not need to repeat them here.

The question behind this particular question is really, "Do you know what you're getting into?" That is to say, how well thought out is your decision to seek a graduate education in social work? A good way to respond to the question is to elaborate on why you chose social work versus other similar professions. For example, someone interested in clinical work with individuals, families, and groups could accomplish the goal by either obtaining an MSW or a doctorate in clinical psychology. In answering this question, that particular individual would have to make the case for why she chose social work over psychology. She might say, for instance, that even though both disciplines offer clinical preparation, the social work option is more attractive to her because of its emphasis on the person-in-environment as opposed to the more individualized psychological perspective.

Write about the other graduate school options you considered along with social work and why you selected social work. Your response will give the committee a clear picture of your understanding of social work. Be clear and to the point. Avoid platitudes such as, "I believe, as does the profession of social work, in the inherent worth of every individual." Instead, get down to the basics of why you think a social work education is better suited for your goals than alternative graduate programs.

You should highlight how you came to learn about social work. Were there specific individuals within the profession who gave you exposure to the profession? Were there particular scholastic or work experiences that fueled your desire to enter the profession of social work? Identify the values that were inherent in those experiences and how they match the values you bring to the profession. In other words, the committee wants to determine if your career goal is well-grounded. Many people write that they are "people people," love working with people, and so they want to be social workers. Anyone can make that statement, but not anyone can fully answer the question posed.

Highlighting Your Experiences

It is most helpful to weave into your narrative specifics about your role within each organization and what you learned from each experience. If space limitations make it necessary to leave out some of the general information about each organization, don't be concerned. The committee is much more interested in *your* experiences and what *you* bring to the school and the profession as a result of *your* experiences than it is in knowing, for example, that a given agency sponsors a New Year's Eve community celebration.

Personal Treatment and Family Experiences

Many people's first experience in social work is as a client. While there is no need for you to provide specifics on your treatment, it is important that it be clear to the committee that whatever issues led you to treatment have been resolved and that you seek entry into the profession to assist others and *not* because you seek to help yourself. Admissions committees are cautious about people who bring their own agenda to the profession. You should be clear that you do not seek entry into the profession to further resolve your own issues.

While a discussion of your own psychotherapy, for example, is relevant, it should avoid excessive self-revelation that may make the admissions committees wonder about your emotional stability. On the other hand, it is quite appropriate to present your own treatment as a tool to learning more about yourself as a fundamental prerequisite to helping others. Also, it reveals a willingness to look at yourself.

A great many applicants select social work as a result of experiences with family members. Again, presenting the situation as a learning experience without excessive revelation is the best approach. For example, it can lead nicely into how the experience led you to seek further exposure to social work as a volunteer.

If the nature of your relative's needs had a substantial impact on your time, the committee will likely ask itself to what extent it may affect your ability to concentrate on graduate work. If the situation persists, you should outline what mechanisms are in place to meet your relative's needs that will allow you time for graduate studies.

Don't Exaggerate or Give the Impression of Exaggerating Experiences

In the quest to be offered admission, it may be tempting to present experiences in a slightly more positive light than perhaps was the case. You certainly want to showcase your experiences and what you learned from them; yet, it is important to present them realistically. It is a fine line to tread. On one hand, you want to state your accomplishments so that the committee understands you bring a valuable background to the school. On the other hand, you do not want to come across as a pretentious applicant who doesn't fully recognize that she has much to learn.

It is wise to not overstate some of the claims of your experiences and accomplishments. The committee is much more interested in applicants who recognize the need for further training than in applicants whose statements indicate they feel very accomplished already.

Question 2: Describe Your Educational Goals and Expectations

The committee wants to know what you hope to gain from your graduate education in social work. Let's look at the question behind the question. The committee is attempting to learn to what extent the program options at its school are congruent with your goals. Most schools of social work have many more applicants than there are places in the class. If an applicant is unclear about her goals or expresses goals that clearly cannot be met by the school's options of study, that applicant may be eliminated from further consideration. For example, the applicant may make a logical and persuasive case for wanting to specialize in rural social work. If the particular school does not offer a rural specialty, the applicant may well be denied admission because the admissions committee believes the school is not in a position to teach the applicant what she wants to learn. Committees look very closely at the "fit" between an applicant's goals and the school's offerings and resources. For example, I recall one applicant to a leading school who had impeccable credentials, yet was denied admission. He stated his primary interest was in international social work, and the committee felt the school did not have the expertise to meet the applicant's needs.

The challenge you face in addressing this question is to demonstrate to the committee that you "did your homework" by learning about the school's options for areas of study concentrations. Clearly state how the program offerings match your goals. It is best not to make statements that appear designed to flatter the school. I advise against a statement such as, "... I would like to undergo training at the best social work department in the Southwest," or "I want to be in the best training program possible." Either of those statements may be interpreted as referring to a school's regional or national ranking. Although such schools are very proud of their rankings (and work very hard to maintain them!), they do not seem to want to be selected by students exclusively on that basis. They'd much rather be selected for the content of the programs than for the ranking itself.

It is also best to avoid platitudes such as "... they (clients) deserve a helping professional prepared through a quality well-balanced program, regardless of its rigors." The committee already knows what clients deserve. It is more interested in learning about the specific reasons you believe its specific school will help you to become a prepared professional.

It is also most important that you make it clear that you want to expand your education, and are not merely seeking a credential.

Your wording should not sound as though it belongs in the pages of a school catalog. Use your own words and say what *you* want to learn in graduate school that you believe will prepare you to do the sort of social work you intend to make your life's work. Connect what you hope to learn at the school to what you hope to do as a practicing professional.

Question 3: Describe Your Short- and Long-term Professional Goals

As much as is possible at this point, you should mention your specific goals. For instance, you may have the objective of becoming a licensed clinical social worker. It is best to avoid drifting off into general statements such as, "... sharing myself as a professional social worker" and "...wanting to have a fulfilling career as a social worker." The committee assumes all applicants want those things. You will serve your cause best by being more specific. What areas of social work are of potential interest to you? How do you see your past experiences (i.e., identify the transferable skills between what you do now and what you hope to do post-master's) and what you hope to obtain from the master's program contributing to your professional work?

Although being as clear as possible about your present professional goals is recommended, this should be tempered with a healthy expectation that other possibilities are likely to arise. Too often, applicants write as though they know precisely what their careers will be. The realization that a graduate education is likely to open her eyes to many new possibilities indicates the applicant understands she has much to learn.

Another way this question is often posed is, "What do you expect to contribute in the future to the profession?" Avoid being vague and making statements of the "baseball, mom, and apple pie" variety. That is, do not make general statements that anyone considering social work might make about wanting to help "..individuals and groups of people no matter who they are, what they do, or where they come from."

Rather than making those types of statements, you'd do better focusing on specifics. With what types of populations, around what issues, and in what settings do you intend to practice? As noted above, you do not want to come across as though you are not open to possibilities that may present themselves in graduate school. To say that you believe the graduate experience may present possibilities you may not yet be aware of would be good.

Question 4: Provide Evidence of Your Capacity for Graduate Work

This question is posed in a number of different ways. For example, you may be asked to write about a social/human problem that interests you.

The intent behind the question is to determine your understanding of a social issue and your perception of the positive and negative forces the profession of social work can bring to bear in addressing the issue. Your response will also serve as a gauge of your level of sophistication in viewing a social work issue and, therefore, your readiness for graduate work. Don't let this alarm you. The committee does not expect you to *have* a graduate-level view of the issue. It only expects you to show *potential* to undertake graduate work. Once again, your writing will be most important. Your ability to explain your position clearly while supporting your views logically and coherently will be examined closely.

Another way to pose this question is, "What does the applicant consider to be a major issue that professional social workers should be concerned with now and in the 21st century; what does the applicant see as a role and responsibility of social work in relation to this issue?"

The point behind the question is to assess the applicant's level of sophistication in viewing social problems. Once again, connecting your educational goals to the offerings of the school would be a good idea. You should select an issue that is related to the population you plan to work with after graduation. For example, if your population of choice is adolescents, you may write about family dysfunction as a result of alcohol and other substance abuse, youth and generational alienation, or another relevant issue. Stay away from generalities and do some serious research on the subject. You can follow with your views on each subject as backed by the facts. Conclude with how you see social work addressing the issue.

It will be beneficial not to be too general in your choice of an issue; after all, this is only one section of your statement. For example, if your interests are in juvenile delinquency and the widening socio-economic gap, you should limit your response to one or the other. Whichever you select, be specific in defining the issue and how you see social work methods as a potential solution. Avoid digressing into side issues that do not address the question.

Do your homework in preparing to write about the issue you select. Be cautious about the claims you make. By doing so, you will avoid the possibility of having your statements disputed if the faculty committee members who happen to read your application are experts on the subject. A faculty expert on your given subject could have some problems with broad generalizations. This is not to say that as an applicant you are expected to be an expert on the subject, but it is expected that you understand your limitations.

Another way the topic of your capacity to undertake graduate work may be addressed is to inquire about the personal qualities you believe you bring to the profession of social work. It is tempting for applicants to highlight strengths while ignoring their areas that would benefit from improvement. It would add a great deal of balance for you to also highlight minimal or non-existent qualities that you hope to develop through your graduate studies and beyond. A social worker must be aware of her shortcomings and identify ways to improve them. That is, after all, what we ask our clients to do. Many applicants make the mistake of tooting their own horns so loudly that they fail to acknowledge that the real purpose of graduate school is to provide an education.

Plans for Covering Expenses

Although not always asked as part of the biographical or personal statement, most schools inquire about the applicant's plans for meeting the expenses of a graduate education. Sometimes it is one of the questions in the application itself.

It is a very important and relevant point. Many schools do not have extensive assistance available, and students will more than likely have to secure scholastic loans and even work part-time while in graduate school. Your response to the question will give the committee a picture of how realistic you are about what you will need to do while in graduate school. If attending school full-time, you will have to carry a full class load and also spend anywhere from sixteen to twenty-four hours per week in a field setting. Above all of that, you will probably need to work between ten and twenty hours per week to supplement your living expenses. If you will be enrolled in a part-time program, you will likely be employed full-time.

If you worked part-time during college, it would be useful to mention it. For example, "I achieved a grade point average of _____ while working 15 hours per week."

Question 5: Describe Why You Seek a Graduate Social Work Education at This Point in Your Career

More often than not, this question is asked only of those applicants who seek a return to school after being employed for some time.

This question seeks to answer the "Why now?" question that all social workers seem to be enamored with (for good reasons). The only really poor answer to this question is to say that you want a master's so you can be promoted. Schools do not want people who are simply seeking a credential. They want people who seek an education.

If your background is in a career unrelated to social work, you need to give the committee a better understanding of (1) how you came to select your present occupation and (2) how, through your time in that profession, you came to recognize social work as your future calling. Was your interest in social work there all along, but you chose the other career for other reasons (financial security or family pressures, for example)? Your statement should answer the important questions the committee asks itself on all career changers: (a) "Why the change?" and (b) "Why now?"

As someone seeking to change careers, you have probably been away from an academic setting for some time. Therefore, your job accomplishments should also be connected to your intellectual capacities, and indirectly to your academic abilities. Some of the same skills that it took to excel in business, for example, skills involved in supervising employees, are very applicable to social work. Some of the same skills that it takes to excel in business, particularly the ones involved in business education programs, are very applicable to the academic setting.

It would be useful for you to highlight how you see the skills you developed in your present career applying to your goals in social work. A great deal will depend on how the committee views your rationale for the career change.

It is tempting for career changers to make passionate, even poetic, arguments for their wish to change careers. In some ways, by so doing they are preaching to the choir. For example, someone switching from business to clinical social work may be tempted to expound on the beauty of clinical practice. The committee does not need to know how different clinical work is from the business environment. Rather, they want to know what qualities the applicant brings to clinical work, the types of clientele she seeks to serve, and how she believes a clinical education at their particular school can help her meet her goals.

It is not necessary to make apologies for having been in another field (you'd be surprised how many people do!), yet you should make a bridge between your previous background and social work. Use examples of how you may have used your skills in volunteer social work settings or with family and friends. Beware, however, that one of the possible dangers of examples of having helped friends and family is that an applicant may unintentionally come across as someone who believes he is a "natural social worker." This sometimes makes admissions committees nervous.

Highlight your awareness that you have much to learn, as you describe how you have helped family and others in the past. Doing so will eliminate the possibility of coming across as someone who thinks he is already a social worker and simply wants a credential. It will help the committee understand that you are seeking an education, not merely some letters to put after your name.

Concluding Your Statement

As mentioned at the beginning of this chapter, many applicants strive to introduce their statements in a clever and unusual way. Equally as many do the same in concluding their statements. Many close by saying how much they hope to be offered admission, how they believe they can make a difference in people's lives, and how intelligent they are (in so many words). Doing so is not necessary, because every applicant hopes to be offered admission, everyone that applies has a sincere belief that they can make a positive difference in people's lives, and all consider themselves intelligent and mature. Rather than saying those things at the end, be thorough in answering the questions, keeping in mind the questions behind the questions, and those things will speak for themselves. By the time the committee reviews your application and reads your statement, it will be the judge of those things.

Going Beyond the Instructions

Just as it is most important to address every point in the statement instructions, it is important not to go beyond what is requested. The old adage of "never volunteer" certainly applies to biographical or personal statements. Making application to graduate schools is a process filled with much anxiety. Many applicants attempt to ease their tension by submitting as many documents as they can think of with their applications. Normally, it is not a good idea to include copies of additional materials. One reason is that the instructions do not state you can do so. The committee may interpret it as a failure to read the directions. Another reason is that the material may hurt instead of help you. For example, applicants sometimes want to include evidence of past work, such as a grant they've authored. Committee persons who review the application may well be some of the nation's foremost experts in grant writing. Will the grant stand up to the scrutiny of such expertise? I believe it would be best not to take that chance.

Helpful Hints

Do...

- begin with a well thought-out introduction (i.e., telling the reader what is ahead).
- consider the questions behind the questions.
- write about the other graduate school options you considered along with social work and why you selected social work.
- provide specifics about your role within each organization and what you learned from each experience.
- when writing about a personal or family crisis, and aspects of the situation persist, you should outline what mechanisms are in place to meet continuing needs that will allow you time for graduate studies.
- clearly state how the school's offerings match your goals *without* making statements that appear designed to flatter the school.
- be as clear as possible about your present professional goals while maintaining a healthy expectation that other possibilities are likely to arise.
- if asked to discuss a social issue, stay away from generalities and do some serious research on the subject.

(continued on next page)

(continued from previous page)

- if asked to discuss the personal qualities you bring to the profession, add balance to your descriptions of your strengths by also highlighting minimal or non-existent qualities that you hope to develop through your graduate studies and beyond.

- if you are changing careers, highlight how you see the skills you developed in your present career applying to your goals in social work.

Don't...

- begin your essay with an overly clever introduction.

- make your essay read like a résumé in narrative form.

- write about personal treatment experiences without making clear to the committee that whatever issues led you to treatment have been resolved and that you seek entry into the profession to assist others and *not* because you seek to help yourself.

- overplay your experiences and risk coming across as a pretentious applicant who doesn't fully recognize that she has much to learn.

- use platitudes such as "I want to give of myself to those in need." Instead, be specific about your goals and how you plan to achieve them.

- conclude by saying how much you hope to be offered admission, how you believe you can make a difference in people's lives, and how intelligent you are (in so many words). Doing so is not necessary.

- go beyond what is requested in the instructions.

Chapter 12

Less Than Perfect Undergraduate Records: What To Do

College can be highly demanding emotionally, intellectually, and financially. In addition, it takes place at a time in most people's lives that has more than its share of stresses. For the so-called traditional student, it comes at the tail end of adolescence, a time of much self exploration and uncertainty. For the so-called non-traditional student who is often also bearing the burden of family responsibilities, it comes at a time when the future looms equally uncertain. Therefore, it is not uncommon for undergraduate records to be less than perfect.

The patterns of uneven undergraduate records are as unique as the students themselves. Generally, however, they fall into three categories. I have often seen undergraduate records that reflect generally above-average performance with the exception of a semester or two of dismal performance. I have also seen records that simply seem to languish in a constant state that exhibits neither academic brilliance nor outright incompetence. I've also come across individuals who have forged excellent careers, yet apologetically explain that their college transcript of a decade ago (or more) is their biggest shame.

Do any of these scenarios (or a combination thereof) mean the end of all hopes for graduate study? Not necessarily. It does mean, however, that you must face the issues head-on in an honest and realistic fashion at the time of your application.

I have seen instances in which applicants rush to provide an explanation after having an application for admission denied. Many schools are reluctant to reverse their decisions except in circumstances in which the information was not available at the time of application and is absolutely compelling. Providing an explanation after the fact usually does not fall into that category, because the explanation could have been offered at the time of initial application. Understandably, schools are hesitant to reopen the process once a denial has been made, for fear of opening the floodgates of requests of appeals from other denied applicants.

Let's look at ways the above three scenarios should be approached.

The Case of Poor Performance During A Brief Period in An Otherwise Above-Average Record

Many applicants make the mistake of not wanting to call attention to a semester or two of poor performance. They carefully avoid all references to it in the hope that the admissions committee will not notice it or, at least, will overlook it. The invariable result is that the committee does notice and, in the absence of any explanation, assumes all was well and the grades in question reflect the student's inability to grasp the material.

A better strategy is to face the issue head on. I recommend what I call a GPA Addendum. It is intended to alert the graduate admissions committee to any unusual circumstances that affected the student's ability to focus on the class materials during the period in question. A good degree of judgment should be exercised in determining to what extent personal matters are discussed. For example, if financial pressures necessitated increasing the amount of work hours, and consequently lessened the amount of time devoted to studies, the family or personal factors at the root of the issue need little elaboration.

A vital part of the Addendum will be the presentation of evidence of (a) how the crisis was resolved and (b) that once the crisis was resolved the student resumed the usual above-average level of performance. Without this last part, the Addendum becomes little more than a poor excuse for deficient performance. The Addendum should be brief, perhaps no more than one-half typewritten page, and present the facts in a straightforward fashion without assuming a "woe is me" tone.

If the application contains a space where you must enter your undergraduate GPA, I recommend placing an asterisk directing the committee to the GPA Addendum. I recommend an Addendum separate from the supplementary or biographical statement, because to include it in the statement may break the flow of expression of the development of your interest in social work, your expectations for a graduate education, and your professional goals.

A sample of a brief, yet effective, Addendum follows. The applicant was offered admission to the school that was his first choice.

I was placed on academic probation during the Summer session and the Fall semester of 1995. I had personal and financial problems which detracted from my studies. In January of 1996 I transferred from the (local) campus of my university to its (main) campus. The reduced cost of living due to facilities such as subsidized married student housing allowed me to adjust my work hours and resume full attention to my studies. I retook the classes I had in the two terms in question and after one semester I was removed from probation having achieved a graduation GPA of 3.47 on a 4.0 scale. I went on to graduate in May of 1998 with a GPA of 3.42.

Letters of Reference

Applicants in this category may be somewhat tempted to obtain "sympathy letters of reference." Such letters are often from clergy, close friends, and similar sources. They typically contain statements of admiration for the endurance displayed by the applicant in difficult times. Although well-meaning, such sources add little of substance to the central issue of informing the committee of the applicant's academic abilities and potential for the profession.

The fact that the applicant overcame the crisis, as evidenced by a return to previous levels of academic excellence, should suffice. There is no reason to dwell on the subject. The letters of reference will be used to best advantage if they come from sources as explained earlier.

Standardized Test Scores

As mentioned earlier, applicants who have an overall above-average undergraduate record should be careful not to allow poor standardized test scores to hurt them. If your scores on the GRE sections average less than 650, you probably should not submit scores if you can help it. Even if you had a period of poor performance in college, that issue was addressed by the resumption of above average performance after the period in question.

An Average to Below-Average Undergraduate GPA

Most graduate schools of social work will require a cumulative or post-sophomore GPA of at least 2.75 on a 4.0 scale. A good number of schools require 3.0 on a 4.0 scale as a minimum.

A word of caution is in order on the meaning of a school's stated minimum GPA. The minimum GPA refers to the lowest GPA with which applicants will be considered for admission. It does not mean that an applicant with a GPA equal to the school's stated minimum is automatically granted admission. For the more competitive programs, there may be few, if any, applicants with undergraduate GPAs equaling the school's stated minimum who are actually offered admission. Rather than attempting to judge your chances of admission based on a school's stated minimum GPA, it is better to inquire of the schools the actual GPA range, mean, median, and mode for those applicants offered admission in the most recent cycle.

In general, if your GPA is below 2.75 on a 4.0 scale, you will probably have difficulties gaining admission to a graduate school of social work. There are, however, a number of strategies you can attempt.

The things you can do will depend largely on how low your GPA is, how much time has elapsed since you completed college, and what you have been doing since graduation. An added factor will be how competitive admissions are to the particular schools of your interest. In general, the higher the ranking of the school, the more competitive the admissions process. Among other factors that will have an impact on your chances of admission will be the number of graduate social work programs that compete for students in your given geographic area and the level of demand for new social workers in the given market.

Current College Seniors and Recent Graduates With a Slightly Lower GPA Than a School's Stated Minimum

If you are in your last year of college and plan to apply for admission to graduate school for next year, your options decrease to the extent that your GPA is below the school's stated minimum.

If you are only slightly below the stated limit (no more than approximately 0.15 below), you may be able to obtain conditional or probationary admission. Be aware, however, that the more prestigious schools, as well as those with extremely high numbers of applicants in relation to the spaces in the incoming class, do not normally grant conditional or probationary admission.

Schools willing to consider probationary admission will pose some stringent requirements. In addition, the number of students admitted on a conditional basis may be no more than a handful in any given school.

If you can make a case that family and work obligations affected your ability to do well in college, your case will be strengthened. By the same token, be ready to present evidence that whatever the circumstances that affected your college performance were, they will be resolved by the time you enter graduate school. If you are unable to provide reasonable evidence that the circumstances will not continue, the admissions committee will have no reason to believe your graduate work will be any better than your undergraduate work.

If your record is mediocre at best throughout college, you will also need to provide additional evidence that you possess the academic abilities necessary for graduate study. Even if someone can substantiate that detrimental circumstances existed during college, it does not necessarily follow that the same individual could have done better had circumstances been better.

Letters of Reference

Whether your overall college performance was only slightly below-average or extremely below-average, I advise against "sympathy letters of reference." As mentioned earlier, aside from retelling your tales of woe, they add little to the real issue at hand. The central question the graduate admissions committee needs answered is, "So, you had unfortunate circumstances during college, but what can you show us to prove you can do well under better circumstances?"

Therefore, I recommend letters of reference from professors where you did your best work. Such letters may show the committee that you have potential, because you managed to do well in some classes despite your circumstances.

Standardized Test Scores

If the school allows the option, submitting credible scores on a standardized test can be a way of providing evidence of your academic abilities and potential for graduate work. Scores from the Graduate Record Examination (GRE) or, for some schools, the Miller Analogies Test (MAT) may be a way to strengthen your application given a low undergraduate GPA. A word of warning, though—as I advised earlier, it is better to wait until after you've received your scores before deciding whether or not to have the scores reported to the schools. True, you will spend a little more money by submitting a request after you take the test, but the expense will be worth it if it keeps average to low scores that can harm your chances of being admitted from being reported.

Each school's definition of a good GRE or MAT score varies depending on the quality of students in its applicant pool. Ask the admissions offices of the schools of your choice what are considered good scores. For the more competitive schools, a score below 650 on each category of the GRE will probably not strengthen your possibilities of admission.

Current College Seniors and Recent Graduates With a GPA Substantially Lower Than a School's Stated Minimum

If you are in your last year of college or graduated from college less than two years before your expected time of entrance into graduate school and your undergraduate GPA is substantially lower than the stated minimum of the schools you hope to attend, your chances of acceptance are low.

For such students, most schools recommend a minimum of two years of successful post-college full-time employment before applying. The two years are recommended because they will test your interest and aptitude for the profession and allow time for natural maturation.

Even after successful employment, however, the academic question will remain. Use the two years to take undergraduate or graduate courses in related fields. Obtaining above-average grades will provide graduate schools with more recent evidence of your abilities and commitment. Be aware that unless those courses are from a graduate school accredited by the Council on Social Work Education, the chances are they will not be transferable for credit once you are formally admitted as a degree-seeking student in a graduate program of social work. Check with the graduate schools you are interested in about the transferability of any classes before enrolling. Even if you find that the classes will not transfer, they will be well worth it if they will help you disprove your previous academic shortcomings.

Possibilities for classes to take include graduate level classes in social work or a related area, such as psychology or sociology, as a non-degree student, or student-at-large. If you did not take courses in research and statistics or in human biology as an undergraduate, this presents an opportunity to meet those and other prerequisites while providing evidence that you can excel academically and that you have the potential for graduate study.

Letters of Reference

The second important advantage to taking student-at-large classes is that you can obtain academic letters of reference from your professors. Good letters can go a long way in laying to rest your earlier college background.

Even with all of the above, generally speaking, if your GPA from college is 2.2 or below on a 4.0 scale, your chances of admission to a graduate program in social work will remain low.

Standardized Test Scores

You may also want to consider taking the Graduate Record Examination (GRE) or the Miller Analogies Test (MAT), if the schools of your interest provide that option, as a way to provide further evidence of academic readiness for graduate school. Be forewarned, however, that even with high grades in student-at-large courses and standardized test scores (depending on how high the scores are), your chances of admission to the highly selective schools may remain low.

If your heart is set on such a school, an alternative is to gain admission to a less selective school and excel in your first year of the graduate program (mostly, if not totally, A grades) and apply to your first choice school as a transfer student for your second year.

There are opposing arguments to this strategy. Arguments against it center mainly around the issue of the continuity of your graduate education. Although curricula in the first year of graduate programs in social work are fairly consistent among schools accredited by the Council on Social Work Education, some philosophical differences among schools lend each program its own particular focus and flavor.

One advantage of this option is that if you are not accepted as a transfer student, you can still complete your Master of Social Work at the school you attended your first year. It is also possible that after spending one year in the school that was not previously your first choice, you may decide you don't want to leave. You may have developed good relationships with your faculty and fellow students and enjoyed the program more than you anticipated.

Distant Past Graduates With a GPA Substantially Lower Than a School's Stated Minimum

If you graduated from college some time ago, depending on how low your GPA was, your academic performance from as long ago as 15 or 20 years may still come back to haunt you.

If you have managed to forge a moderately successful career, perhaps one of the biggest obstacles you will encounter will be facing the ghost of your past. Many a highly successful and normally confident professional seems to lose composure upon touching on the subject of a distant past poor college record. In fact, many delay seeking an advanced degree to avoid battle with the old dragon of their past shortcomings. Once they decide to accept the challenge, most are successful in slaying the dragon. This is not to say, however, that victory comes without substantial effort.

Don't hesitate to apply the skills that have made you a professional success to the admissions process. Actively seek interviews with admissions personnel at the schools of your choice. Use the interview to highlight your maturity and skills and how they relate to your decision to seek graduate education, as well as ways they will contribute to your post-graduate goals. Be matter-of-fact about your college record without being apologetic. Chances are the interviewer recalls younger days when the long-term implications of a college record were not considered.

It is important to approach the interviews as a means to learn what each institution will require of you to address the academic prerequisites for admission. It is best, and more realistic, not to approach the interviews with the goal of convincing officials that your professional record is so outstanding as to negate the need to address the academic issues. If you do, the likely result will be that you leave the impression of being egotistical and lacking understanding of the unique qualities and skills necessary for academic success.

Even despite an applicant's highly successful professional record, schools will require some recent evidence of academic success. I have seen extremely successful individuals react in shock to being denied admission to graduate school because they failed to provide evidence of recent academic success. The reason graduate schools need to see such evidence is that skills required for professional success and those required for academic success are not always the same. To offer a more mundane example, even Michael Jordan—with all his athletic talents—could not transfer his success on the basketball court to the baseball diamond.

I recommend the same strategies offered in the previous several pages. One strategy is to take some graduate level classes as a student-at-large. They will provide graduate schools with recent evidence of your academic abilities. Just as important, they will serve to ease your readjustment to the role of student. If your professional position allows you independence and responsibility over others, adjusting to the role of student may be more emotionally challenging than you think. It will be a humbling experience indeed to be in a classroom with people half your age who seem, at least initially, much more capable than you.

Standardized tests such as the Graduate Record Examination (GRE) and Miller Analogies Test (MAT) are also ways to build up your academic credentials, provided the schools of your choice accept standardized test scores. The same warnings and caveats about how to prepare for standardized tests and how to decide when and which scores to have sent to graduate schools explained earlier in this *Guide* apply to you.

Keep in mind that the more highly ranked schools may be more difficult to enter. Interestingly, the highly ranked schools may also be more flexible in evaluating the unique backgrounds and qualifications of non-traditional students. You may also want to consider the option of going to a school that ranks lower in your list of preferences and attempting to transfer for your second year to the school you rank as your number one choice.

Helpful Hints

Do...

- face issues of past academic short-comings honestly and realistically at the time of your application.
- use an addendum to your application to alert the graduate admissions committee to any unusual circumstances that affected your ability to focus on your studies during a period of poor performance in college.
- follow explanations of periods of poor academic performance with evidence of a return to previous levels of academic excellence.
- consider using standardized test scores to provide evidence of academic ability if your undergraduate record was average to poor.
- if your college record is extremely poor, consider taking graduate level classes in social work or a related area, such as psychology or sociology, as a non-degree student to show current evidence of academic ability.

Don't...

- avoid all references to brief periods of poor academic college performance in the hope that the admissions committee will not notice it or overlook it.
- submit "sympathy letters of reference."

Chapter 13

You're Accepted: What's Next?

You may just be getting started now, but, given the right research and preparation, the day will come when offers of admission will come to your mailbox. When they do, celebrate and pat yourself on the back for a job well done. Once the celebration is over, however, it will be time to consider your options carefully. The factors to consider will include the timing of each offer relative to offers from other schools (and which school is your first choice) and relative to the financial aid award, whether the offer is for an actual place in the class or to be placed on a school's waiting list, and whether your personal circumstances have changed and you wish to pursue deferring your admission to a future academic year.

Timing of The Offer

Most schools process applications for admission before proceeding to make financial aid awards. Therefore, you will probably receive offers of admission and be asked to accept or reject the offer before you know the level of financial aid you are awarded. Accepting an offer usually entails making a substantial cash deposit anywhere between $100 and $500 to hold your place in the class. To add to the dilemma, acceptance deposits are usually nonrefundable. Basically, it is like being asked whether or not you want to buy something before you know the price.

It is a difficult decision to make. You may have an offer from the school of your dreams but you may not yet know whether you can afford to go there. If the school in question is private and the financial aid award is good, chances are that the amount you pay will be roughly equivalent to the amount you would pay at a public university in the same state. If the award is at a lower level, however, you could pay dearly for accepting without knowing the amount of the award first.

Students who find themselves in that difficult position often opt to request an extension of the time allotted to accept or decline the offer. Some schools are reluctant to grant an extension, while others do so routinely. You have nothing to lose by trying.

Waiting Lists

An added dilemma confronts students who are placed on a school's waiting list. They are told that they qualify for admission but the class is full. If the notice comes from a school you are very interested in, it is very tempting to pass up solid offers of admission from other schools in the hope that a spot opens up and you are selected from the waiting list.

Before you decide to pass up other offers, ask for more specifics about the chances of being selected for an open spot from the waiting list. Inquire how many people are on the waiting list and how many spots are expected to open. Generally, schools make more offers of admission than there are places in the class. They "overbook" the class based on past experience of the number of offers of admission that are usually declined. Therefore, spots will usually only open up for waiting list candidates if the schools underestimated the rate of decline responses.

Another question to ask is at what place you are on the waiting list. Are you the next person or the tenth next person on the list? Chances are that the waiting list is not a list but a waiting pool. That is, people are not ranked within the group. As openings arise, people are selected not based solely on the rating of their applications but on other factors. For instance, the school may want to balance its male-female ratio or the number of students who expect to be in different concentrations and make waiting list selections accordingly.

Perhaps the most important question to ask is what effect getting a spot so late will mean to your financial aid award. Will there still be enough money left?

My best advice if you are on a waiting list is, unless you have a fairly solid idea that your chances are good to get a spot in the class, don't pass up other offers. You could wind up with no school to attend and have to start all over again the following year.

Deferring Admission

Some schools allow admitted applicants to defer the date of admission for periods of one to two years. For example, if the applicant is offered admission for Autumn of 2000, he can defer the start of school until Autumn of 2001 or even Autumn of 2002. Policies on deferral vary among schools, and it is best to consult individual schools.

If a school allows you that option, there are pluses and minuses you should consider. Having an additional year or two of full-time employment in social service will certainly benefit you. It will give you a nice foundation for graduate work. You will have more of a real-world frame to fit the theories you will learn in the classroom. During your year to two years of employment, you will enjoy the peace of mind of knowing that you have been admitted and have a place in a graduate school.

Some people use the option of deferral to spend time in the Peace Corps or in other similar programs. There are many excellent experiences you may not be able to enjoy later in your life. Having a place assured in a graduate school allows for concentrating on the experience without having to mail application materials from faraway lands where mail service may not be reliable.

A possible disadvantage to deferring admission is cost. Tuition rates have been steadily rising at rates well above inflation for a good number of years. Therefore, the cost of your education will be greater as time goes on. With a one-year deferral, the total cost of your graduate education may rise as much as ten percent and even more if you defer for two years. In addition, financial aid benefits are in a period of decline. Many educational institutions are experiencing periods of financial difficulties, and this is being reflected in financial aid policies.

Chances are that financial aid packages will be smaller as the years progress. Full-tuition scholarships even for the most gifted applicants are, for the most part, a thing of the past. The gap between ever-increasing tuition rates and decreasing financial aid packages is likely to grow wider. Unfortunately for most students, the gap must be bridged through educational loans and other personal and family resources. Purely on economic grounds, I suggest attending graduate school as soon as possible.

Many schools, on the other hand, do not allow students to defer admission. Some schools in this group may allow reapplication for a period of up to two years without requiring a reapplication fee. In addition, the reapplication procedure may be much simpler than was the case for the original application. For instance, the application form may be much shorter. Resubmission of transcript and other information that will remain unchanged may not be necessary. A brief update to your biographical statement indicating your activities since the time of the original application and perhaps one or two additional letters of reference may suffice.

A very important point is not to take readmission for granted. It is not uncommon for reapplicants to be denied admission, even though they may have been offered admission the first time. For any given school, the quality of the applicant pool varies somewhat from year to year. If a person was a marginal applicant, a slight increase in the quality of the applicant pool could cause a denial.

In addition, many unpredictable and highly subjective factors may come into play. When all is said and done, the fate of an applicant may rest on factors as unpredictable and subjective as who happens to be the person or persons on the admissions committee who read the application. Members have different perspectives and, in some cases, may view the same applicant in very different ways. A more thorough discussion of admissions committees may be found in the introduction to Part II of this book.

Accepting the Offer

Once all is said and done and you've made the final choice of school, it is time to accept the offer. If you were thorough in your contacts and visit, the admissions office probably knows you by now. In accepting the offer, I recommend that you display the same sense of thoroughness and professionalism that you showed in your search. The mechanics of accepting the offer may be as simple as checking off a line on a form sent to you by the school. If that is the case, you should definitely comply with the instructions and complete the form. Nevertheless, I recommend you also include a cover letter indicating your acceptance, addressing any remaining items, asking whatever questions you may have about what is next, and thanking the office of admissions for their assistance through the application process. You would be surprised how few people thank admissions staff and how much it is appreciated. A nice brief letter as follows would be appropriate:

I am in receipt of your letter dated March 16, 2000 offering me admission to your Autumn, 2000 entering class as well as a Dean's Scholarship in the amount of $6,000.00 (renewable per your requirements).

I am very pleased to accept your offer and enclose a check in the amount of $400.00 as deposit on tuition. I have requested my undergraduate institution to send official final transcripts directly to you at the close of my last semester this June.

Thank you very much for all your kind assistance and patience during the application process and your hospitality during my visit. I look forward very much to being a student at your school.

A question often asked by students who are soon to begin graduate school is if there are any books or other materials they should be reading before beginning school. My response surprises many of them. I encourage them to relax and enjoy their summer (or whatever time remains before classes begin). The application process is rigorous, filled with many important decisions, and provokes much anxiety. Now that you have lived through it, you deserve a hearty congratulations and some time for yourself. The time remaining is much better spent relaxing than in attempts to further prepare for school. If you weren't prepared, the school would not have accepted you. There will be plenty of reading to do once school begins. There is no need to jump into the frying pan before your time.

If you are coming to your graduate school from another city, I recommend you arrive at least four to seven days before the beginning of school. Doing so will allow you the opportunity to become familiar with your new surroundings and get to know a few people on campus. Adjusting to the pace of graduate school will be more manageable if you've had the opportunity to get to know the basics of your new setting before classes begin.

Most schools host some kind of welcoming reception, picnic, or other event. In many cases, the event represents a substantial expense for the school. In today's climate of shrinking budgets, schools still recognize the importance of a good beginning for new students. Don't underestimate the importance and the many benefits of attending. It will allow you to meet faculty, staff, second-year or more advanced students, and your fellow classmates. The relationships you begin to form will be an invaluable support through graduate school and, in many cases, throughout your career.

Helpful Hints

Do...

- consider what the "true cost" of a particular school will be by looking at your net cost after financial aid is known.
- follow to the letter all financial aid requirements and deadlines.
- ask precisely what it means if you're placed on a school's "waiting list."
- consider the pluses and minuses if you are considering deferring admission.
- send a cover letter with your acceptance.
- make time for yourself before school begins.
- (if you are from out of town) arrive to campus a few days early.
- CONGRATULATE YOURSELF!

Don't...

- let the cost of a given school be the sole determinant of whether to seek admission.
- jump at the first offer of admission; consider other offers (and how each compares in financial assistance).
- forget to thank admissions staff.
- underestimate the importance of making friends among faculty, staff, and other students.

Chapter 14

The Doctoral Decision

For most purposes, the master's is considered the terminal degree in the profession of social work. In 1996, according to the Council on Social Work Education, the number of students enrolled in doctoral programs was approximately 6% that of students enrolled in master's programs. Nevertheless, even if at this point you are only contemplating seeking a master's degree, there are factors you should know about the doctoral option.

What Can You Do with a Doctorate That You Cannot Do with a Master's Degree?

The short answer to that question is "not much." The more complete answer, of course, is much more complicated. Let's focus on the short answer first. Master's trained social workers (for purposes of this chapter, defined as master's level social workers who do not also have doctoral training) are found in all areas of the profession, including direct practice, administration, teaching, and research. In short, there are no areas of practice reserved exclusively for doctoral degree holders. The more complicated answer involves the fact that having doctoral training most certainly enhances the ability to practice and advance in certain practice areas.

Most notable are the areas of research and teaching. Whereas master's trained social workers engage in both of those activities, their counterparts with doctoral training generally hold an advantage. Most doctoral programs of social work have as their primary mission to prepare researchers. Master's programs, on the other hand, have as their mission to train practitioners. Therefore, doctorate holders generally have a more thorough knowledge of research methods than their master's trained counterparts. Research and teaching go hand in hand, particularly in the larger academic settings.

Council on Social Work Education figures for 1996 highlight the importance of a doctorate to achieving tenured status. In schools with master's and baccalaureate programs, 90.5% of professors, 83.6% of associate professors, and 62.3% of assistant professors held doctoral degrees in social work or other fields. Faculty with master's degrees, on the other hand, tended to hold the majority of non-tenured slots (85.7% of instructors, 76.6% of lecturers, and 77.1% of other non-tenured positions). In schools with only baccalaureate programs, the figures were lower but still significant. In those programs, 71.8% of professors, 54.7% of associate professors, and 40.8% of assistant professors held doctorates—90.7% of instructors, 89% of lecturers, and 88% of other non-tenured positions held master's degrees.

If your full-time goal is academia, you should consider doctoral training. On the other hand, if you wish to teach as a supplement to a more practice-oriented professional life, a master's degree will suffice.

These figures may make you feel that many years of schooling lie ahead if your goal is academia. The prospect may appear particularly daunting if you are at an early point in your career, either about to finish college or recently graduated, and are exploring master's programs. It may help for you to know that most doctoral students have spent a good number of years working at the master's level before returning to school. In 1996, 79.9% of full-time doctoral students were age 31 and over (42.4% of those were 41 and over) and 93.7% of part-time doctoral students were 31 and over (61.5% over 41). Forty-six percent of doctoral students were enrolled part time.

The Cost of a Doctoral Education

For full-time doctoral students, the larger cost of a doctoral education is the income they forego from full-time employment. Whereas 58% of master's program students in 1996 reported having student loans, only 6.1% of doctoral students took student loans. The difference is that 40.4% of doctoral students held research and graduate assistantships (which often include tuition and fees) whereas only 3.7% of master's students held such positions. Figures are not available for financial aid of part-time doctoral students. It is likely, however, that their full-time income results in higher out-of-pocket costs.

What Do You Look for in a Doctoral Program?

Unlike master's programs, doctoral programs are not accredited by the Council on Social Work Education. Therefore, there is a much wider variation in the content, focus, and overall quality of programs. That means that students shopping for a doctoral program must be much more careful.

With some variations, most doctoral programs focus on research. The focus of the research is likely to vary according to (a) the overall emphasis of the school and (b) the expertise represented on the faculty. As noted in the discussion of master's programs elsewhere in this book, most schools have developed a particular perspective over time. There are schools, for instance, that focus heavily on policy and administration aspects of social work, while others have a clinical perspective. The historical focus of the school affects the school's selection of faculty, which, in turn, preserves and enhances the school's focus. Therefore, a key factor to explore is the match between your area of interest and that of the schools you are considering.

A beginning master's student does not need to know precisely her intended area of social work practice. After all, a master's student has most of the first half of the master's program to explore social work through the core curriculum required by the

Council on Social Work Education. A doctoral applicant, however, is expected to have a fairly clear idea of her intended area of research. Although most doctoral programs begin with a block of courses, there are usually only a handful of required courses. The rest are selected by the student in preparation for the dissertation phase. The first task for a prospective doctoral applicant is to define as clearly as possible the subject area that is to be the main thrust of her doctoral studies.

Once an area is identified, a close review of faculty interests among various schools is in order. Does the school have a core of faculty conducting research in the area of your interest? If so, read as much of their work as possible. My advice to prospective doctoral applicants to the School of Social Service Administration of the University of Chicago while I was assistant dean there was to behave as a doctoral student while an applicant. That is, do your research. Know the work of the faculty and whether it matches your interests.

The next step is to visit the schools you are considering and meet with faculty to discuss their work and your interests. Are they willing to work with doctoral students as advisors or chairs of dissertation committees? Look beyond their scholarly qualities to their human qualities. Are they people with whom you would enjoy working? The most successful doctoral experiences result from mentoring relationships developed with faculty. Also inquire about their research plans for the next four to six years. Do their plans include a change of focus that may not match your needs? Do their plans include extensive periods on sabbatical or as visiting faculty elsewhere? Many doctoral educations are prolonged because students must work long-distance with dissertation committee members.

Meeting with current doctoral students is also critical. Do they find the faculty and overall climate of the school supportive of doctoral students? Many schools devote their resources to enhancing baccalaureate and master's programs to the detriment of doctoral programs. Doctoral programs generally cost money for schools, whereas baccalaureate and master's programs generate money. Most doctoral programs are small, accepting anywhere from only 8 or 10 to perhaps 20 new students each year. Add to those numbers the fact that students take only a handful of common courses and quickly disperse into courses specific to their areas of interest and disperse further into their respective dissertation areas. That means that the doctoral experience can be a lonely one. Are there associations of doctoral students within the social work program or the university at large? Do not underestimate the importance of a supportive group of peers.

In short, what a doctoral applicant should look for in a school is as diverse as the population of prospective applicants. The best advice is to know exactly what you seek and look for a program that best matches your goals.

What Do Doctoral Programs Look for in Applicants?

Aside from a clearly defined area of interest as described above, doctoral programs look for evidence of academic preparation and potential for advanced studies, professional maturity, and a commitment to research. With some variations, applications require undergraduate and graduate transcripts, a personal statement, samples of writing (preferably research), and letters of recommendation. The key factor to highlight in all of these is evidence of experience and potential for research.

Academic preparation is measured by the quality of the applicant's academic performance in the master's and baccalaureate programs. A brilliant graduate record does not necessarily negate a poor undergraduate record. In fact, baccalaureate achievement is often seen as a better predictor of doctoral performance than the graduate record. An argument for this view is that advanced undergraduate courses are more purely academic than MSW courses, which tend to be more practice oriented. Evidence of above average achievement in research and writing is fundamental.

Seeking a doctoral degree in any field represents an enormous commitment. Most social workers do not choose to do it because, as noted earlier, the MSW is sufficient for most purposes. A few, however, undertake the task. When viewed in terms of the representation of doctoral degree holders in academia, the impact of these relatively few is great on the profession. Beyond teaching itself, their impact on informing practitioners through their research is also great. Whereas most top-level administrators in public and private social agencies are master's trained, most recognize the importance of seeking doctoral consultants from academia and elsewhere.

Helpful Hints

Do...

- have a clearly defined area of interest.
- read thoroughly the writings of faculty in programs you are considering.
- meet with faculty to evaluate their interest in and availability for working with doctoral students.
- meet with current doctoral students to learn firsthand the pluses and minuses of each particular program.

Don't...

- overlook the human element of faculty (is the "chemistry" right between you?).
- fail to realize research is the name of the game in doctoral programs.
- underestimate the time cost of undertaking a doctoral education.

Part III

Sources For Your Search

SOURCES FOR YOUR SEARCH

This section is intended to provide you with resources in locating a program that meets your needs. It is also intended to provide you with sources to inform you about the requirements in the state or states where you may be residing after completing graduate school.

The first portion of this section is devoted to a list of accredited master's degree social work programs and MSW programs currently in candidacy in the United States. Programs are listed alphabetically by state. In addition to listing each program's postal address, Web site addresses are listed for those programs that have them.

In visiting the Web sites of the various schools, it is also every bit as important to visit the Web page for the host institution. As noted earlier in this Guide, *understanding the host institution can yield insight into the school itself. All schools' Web sites have a link to their host university Web site. If the school you are considering does not currently have a Web site listed here, it would be helpful to locate the host university's Web page. Many schools may not have a Web site at the time of the writing of this book but may have one by the time you are reading it. A list of all U.S. university and college web pages may be found at:* http://dir.yahoo.com/Education/Higher_Education/Colleges_and_Universities/United_States/Complete_Listing/

The second portion of this section is a compilation of the results of a survey that was sent to the accredited schools and schools in candidacy for accreditation. Sixty-seven schools responded to the survey, providing insight into what they see as unique aspects of their schools, what student organizations their schools have to offer, and what they see as important points for applicants to consider.

The third part of this section consists of a list of boards for social work licensing and certification for all fifty states, the District of Columbia, Puerto Rico, and the Virgin Islands. Knowing the licensing or certification guidelines of the states where you may be residing after graduate school will help you make a more informed decision about the program that will best prepare and qualify you for the type of social work you intend to practice.

All qualifying examinations in all states and territories are administered by the American Association of State Social Work Boards (AASSWB). This organization is the best source of information for questions on reciprocity among states and the categories of examination required by each state. Each state listing includes the levels of practice licensed and the education, experience, and examination requirements for each.

This is followed by an Application Tracking Form you may wish to use to record information on each school to which you are making application as you proceed through the application process.

Finally, this section includes a list of questions to ask when you visit schools, a worksheet for the biographical statement, and a listing of sources of further information.

Use these materials to organize your efforts as you make your way through the application process.

Appendix A

Master of Social Work Programs Accredited by the Council on Social Work Education

The material in Appendix A and Appendix B is reprinted with permission of the Council on Social Work Education. The information is current as of September 1999.

Alabama
Alabama A & M University
Graduate Social Work Department
P.O. Box 302
Normal, AL 35762
Shelley A. Wyckoff, Chair
Rebecca Buckner, Coordinator
256-851-5475
FAX 256-851-5484
http://www.aamu.edu/

University of Alabama
School of Social Work
Box 870314
Tuscaloosa, AL 35487-0314
Lucinda Lee Roff, Dean
Carol Drolen, Master's Program Director
205-348-7027
FAX 205-348-9419
http://www.ua.edu/socwork/index.htm

Alaska
University of Alaska, Anchorage
School of Social Work
College of Health, Education, and Social Welfare
3211 Providence Drive
Anchorage, AK 99508-8230
Elizabeth A. Sirles, Director
907-786-6907
FAX 907-786-6912
http://www.uaa.alaska.edu/socwork/

Arizona
Arizona State University
School of Social Work
Box 871802
Tempe, AZ 85287-1802
Elizabeth A. Segal, Interim Director
480-965-2795
FAX 480-965-2799
http://ssw.asu.edu/

Arkansas
University of Arkansas at Little Rock
School of Social Work
2801 S. University
Little Rock, AR 72204
Howard M. Turney, Director
501-569-3240
FAX 501-569-3184
http://www.ualr.edu/~swdept/

California

California State University, Fresno
Department of Social Work Education
5310 Campus Drive
M/S 102
Fresno, CA 93740-8019
G. "Vishu" Visweswaran, Director
559-278-3992
FAX 559-278-7191
http://www.csufresno.edu/

California State University, Long Beach
Department of Social Work
1250 Bellflower Boulevard
Long Beach, CA 90840-0902
John Oliver, Director
Linda McCracken, Coordinator
562-985-7774
FAX 562-985-5514
http://www.csulb.edu/

California State University, Sacramento
Division of Social Work
6000 J Street
Sacramento, CA 95819-6090
Joseph Anderson, Director
916-278-6943
FAX 916-278-7167
http://www.hhs.csus.edu/SW/

California State University, San Bernardino
Department of Social Work
5500 University Parkway
San Bernardino, CA 92407
Teresa Morris, Director
909-880-5501
FAX 909-880-7029
http://ssbs.csusb.edu/social_work/

California State University, Stanislaus
Master of Social Work Department
801 W. Monte Vista Avenue
Turlock, CA 95382
Ellen Dunbar, Director
209-667-3091
FAX 209-667-3869
http://www.csustan.edu/Social_Work/index.htm

Loma Linda University
Master of Social Work Program
Department of Social Work
Griggs Hall
Loma Linda, CA 92350
Beverly J. Buckles, Chair
909-478-8550
FAX 909-478-4450
http://www.llu.edu/llu/

San Diego State University
School of Social Work
5500 Campanile Drive
San Diego, CA 92182-4119
Anita S. Harbert, Director
619-594-6865
FAX 619-594-5991
http://www-rohan.sdsu.edu/dept/chhs/sw/sw.html

San Francisco State University
School of Social Work
1600 Holloway Avenue
San Francisco, CA 94132
Marvin D. Feit, Director
415-338-1003
FAX 415-338-0591
http://www.sfsu.edu/

San Jose State University
College of Social Work
One Washington Square
Suite 215
San Jose, CA 95192-0124
Sylvia R. Andrew, Dean
408-924-5800
FAX 408-924-5892
http://www.sjsu.edu/depts/SocialWork/

University of California at Berkeley
School of Social Welfare

120 Haviland Hall
Berkeley, CA 94720-7400
James Midgley, Dean
510-642-5039
FAX 510-643-6126
http://hav54.socwel.berkeley.edu/

University of California at Los Angeles
Department of Social Welfare
School of Public Policy and Social Research
3250 Public Policy Building
Box 951656
Los Angeles, CA 90095-1656
A. E. Benjamin, Chair
310-825-2892
FAX 310-206-7564
http://www.sppsr.ucla.edu/acad/sw/aca_sw.html

University of Southern California
School of Social Work
MRF Building, Room 214
699 W. 34th Street
Los Angeles, CA 90089-0411
Marilyn Flynn, Dean
213-740-2711
FAX 213-740-3301
http://www.usc.edu/dept/socialwork/

Colorado

Colorado State University
Department of Social Work
127 Education Building
Fort Collins, CO 80523-1586
Ben P. Granger, Head
970-491-1893
FAX 970-491-7280
http://www.colostate.edu/Depts/SocWork/

University of Denver
Graduate School of Social Work
2148 S. High Street
Denver, CO 80208-2886
Catherine F. Alter, Dean
303-871-2886
FAX 303-871-2845
http://www.du.edu/gssw/gsswnav.htm

Connecticut

Southern Connecticut State University
Graduate Social Work Program
Department of Social Work
101 Farmham Avenue
New Haven, CT 06515
Elbert Siegel, Director
Mark Senzer, Graduate Program Coordinator
203-392-6560
FAX 203-392-6580
http://www.southernct.edu/

University of Connecticut
School of Social Work
1798 Asylum Avenue
West Hartford, CT 06117
Kay Davidson, Dean
860-570-9141
FAX 860-570-9264
http://www.socialwork.uconn.edu/

Delaware

Delaware State University
Master of Social Work Program
Department of Social Work
1200 N. DuPont Highway
Dover, DE 19901
John N. Austin, Chair
302-857-6770
FAX 302-857-6794
http://www.dsc.edu/

District of Columbia

Catholic University of America
National Catholic School of Social Service
Shahan Hall-Cardinal Station
Washington, DC 20064
Ann Patrick Conrad, Dean
202-319-5454
FAX 202-319-5093
http://ncsss.cua.edu/

Gallaudet University
Department of Social Work
800 Florida Avenue NE
Washington, DC 20002-3695
Janet L. Pray, Director
202-651-5160
FAX 202-651-5817
http://www.gallaudet.edu/~swweb/

Howard University
School of Social Work
601 Howard Place NW
Washington, DC 20059
Richard A. English, Dean
202-806-7300
FAX 202-387-4309
http://www.socialwork.howard.edu/

Florida
Barry University
School of Social Work
11300 N.E. 2nd Avenue
Miami Shores, FL 33161
Stephen M. Holloway, Dean
305-899-3900
FAX 305-899-3934
http://www2.barry.edu/vpaa-ssw/default.htm

Florida International University
School of Social Work
AC-1 Building, Suite 234
3000 N.E. 151st Street
North Miami, FL 33181-3600
Ray Thomlison, Director
305-919-5880
FAX 305-919-5313
http://www.fiu.edu/~cupa/social-work.html

Florida State University
School of Social Work
UCC 2505
Tallahassee, FL 32306-2570
Dianne H. Montgomery, Dean
850-644-4751
FAX 850-644-9750
http://ssw.fsu.edu/

University of Central Florida
School of Social Work
P.O. Box 163358
Orlando, FL 32828
Mary Van Hook, Director
407-823-2114
FAX 407-823-5697
http://www.cohpa.ucf.edu/social/

University of South Florida
School of Social Work
MGY 132
4202 E. Fowler Avenue
Tampa, FL 33620-8100
Jean Amuso, Director
813-974-1362
FAX 813-974-4675
http://www.cas.usf.edu/social_work/index.html

Georgia
Clark Atlanta University
School of Social Work
James P. Brawley Drive at Fair Street S.W.
Atlanta, GA 30314-4391
Dorcas Davis Bowles, Dean
404-880-8548
FAX 404-880-6434
http://www.cau.edu/

University of Georgia
School of Social Work
Tucker Hall
Athens, GA 30602
Bonnie Yegidis, Dean
706-542-5424
FAX 706-542-3845
http://www.ssw.uga.edu/

Valdosta State University
Division of Social Work
1500 Patterson Street
Valdosta, GA 31698
Peggy H. Cleveland, Director
912-249-4864
FAX 912-245-4341

http://www.valdosta.peachnet.edu/sowk/

Hawaii

University of Hawaii at Manoa
School of Social Work
2500 Campus Road
Honolulu, HI 96822
Patricia L. Ewalt, Dean
808-956-6300
FAX 808-956-5964
http://www2.hawaii.edu/sswork/welcome.html

Idaho

Boise State University
School of Social Work
1910 University Drive
Boise, ID 83725
Juanita Hepler, Director
Martha Wilson, Coordinator
208-426-1568
FAX 208-426-4291
http://www.idbsu.edu/socwork/

Illinois

Aurora University
George Williams College
School of Social Work
347 S. Gladstone Avenue
Aurora, IL 60506-4892
Sandra Alcorn, Dean
630-844-5419
FAX 630-844-4923
http://www.aurora.edu/

Loyola University of Chicago
School of Social Work
820 N. Michigan Avenue
Chicago, IL 60611
Joseph A. Walsh, Dean
312-915-7005
FAX 312-915-7645
http://www.luc.edu/schools/socialwork/

Southern Illinois University at Carbondale
School of Social Work
Quigley Hall, Room 4
Mail Code 4329
Carbondale, IL 62901-4329
Martin B. Tracy, Director
618-453-2243
FAX 618-453-1219
http://www.siu.edu/~socwork/

University of Chicago
School of Social Service Administration
969 E. 60th Street
Chicago, IL 60637
Edward F. Lawlor, Dean
773-702-1420
FAX 773-834-1582
http://www.ssa.uchicago.edu/

University of Illinois at Chicago
Jane Addams College of Social Work
M/C 309
1040 W. Harrison Street
Chicago, IL 60607-7134
Creasie Finney Hairston, Dean
312-996-3219
FAX 312-996-1802
http://www.uic.edu/jaddams/college/

University of Illinois at Urbana-Champaign
School of Social Work
1207 W. Oregon Street
Urbana, IL 61801
Jill Doner Kagle, Dean
217-333-2261
FAX 217-244-5220
http://www.social.uiuc.edu/

Indiana

Indiana University/Purdue University at Indianapolis
School of Social Work
902 W. New York Street
ES 4138
Indianapolis, IN 46202-5156
Sheldon Siegel, Dean

Marion Wagner, Director
317-274-6705
FAX 317-274-8630
http://iussw.iupui.edu/

Branches

Indiana University: Northwest Campus
Raintree Hall Room 213
3400 Broadway
Gary, IN 46408
Grafton H. Hull, Jr., Director
219-981-4266
FAX 219-981-4264
http://iussw.iupui.edu/

Indiana University: South Bend Campus
1700 Mishawaka Avenue
P.O. Box 7111
South Bend, IN 46634-7111
Paul Newcomb, Director
219-237-4880
FAX 219-237-4876
http://iussw.iupui.edu/

University of Southern Indiana
Social Work Department
8600 University Boulevard
Evansville, IN 47712
David Westhuis, Director
812-464-1843
FAX 812-465-1116
http://www.usi.edu/EDU/SOC_WORK/SOCIAL.HTM

Iowa

University of Iowa
School of Social Work
308 North Hall
Iowa City, IA 52242-1223
Salome Raheim, Director
319-335-1250
FAX 319-335-1711
http://www.uiowa.edu/~socialwk/

Kansas

University of Kansas
School of Social Welfare
Twente Hall
Lawrence, KS 66045-2510
Ann Weick, Dean
785-864-4720
FAX 785-864-5277
http://www.socwel.ukans.edu/

Washburn University
Department of Social Work
1700 College Avenue
Topeka, KS 66621
Nancie Palmer, Chair
785-231-1010 ext.1616
FAX 785-231-1027
http://www.washburn.edu/sas/sw/index.html

Kentucky

University of Kentucky
College of Social Work
619 Patterson Office Tower
Lexington, KY 40506-0027
Kay Hoffman, Dean
606-257-6654
FAX 606-323-1030
http://www.uky.edu/SocialWork/welcome.html

University of Louisville
Raymond A. Kent School of Social Work
Oppenheimer Hall
Louisville, KY 40292
Terry L. Singer, Dean
502-852-3944
FAX 502-852-0422
http://www.louisville.edu/kent/

Louisiana

Louisiana State University
School of Social Work
Huey P. Long Field House

Baton Rouge, LA 70803
Kenneth I. Millar, Dean
225-388-1351
FAX 225-388-1357
http://www.socialwork.lsu.edu/

Southern University at New Orleans
School of Social Work
6400 Press Drive
New Orleans, LA 70126
Millie M. Charles, Dean
504-286-5376
FAX 504-286-5387
http://www.suno.edu/

Tulane University
School of Social Work
6823 St. Charles Avenue
New Orleans, LA 70118-5672
Suzanne E. England, Dean
504-865-5314
FAX 504-862-8727
http://www.tulane.edu/~tssw/

Maine
University of Maine
School of Social Work
5770 Social Work Building
Orono, ME 04469
Gail Werrbach, Director
207-581-2387
FAX 707-581-2396
http://www.ume.maine.edu/~soclwork/

University of New England
School of Social Work
11 Hills Beach Road
Biddeford, ME 04005
Joanne J. Thompson, Director
207-283-0171
FAX 207-284-7633
http://www.une.edu/chp/ssw/sswhome.htm

Maryland
University of Maryland at Baltimore
School of Social Work
Louis L. Kaplan Hall
525 W. Redwood Street
Baltimore, MD 21201-1777
Jesse J. Harris, Dean
410-706-7794
FAX 410-706-0273
http://ssw.umaryland.edu/

Massachusetts
Boston College
Graduate School of Social Work
McGuinn Hall
140 Commonwealth Avenue
Chestnut Hill, MA 02467-3807
June Gary Hopps, Dean
617-552-4290
FAX 617-552-3199
http://www.bc.edu/bc_org/avp/gssw/gssw.htm

Boston University
School of Social Work
264 Bay State Road
Boston, MA 02215
Wilma Peebles-Wilkins, Dean
617-353-3750
FAX 617-353-5612
http://www.bu.edu/ssw/

Salem State College
School of Social Work
352 Lafayette Street
Salem, MA 01970
Donald P. Riley, Director
978-542-6650
FAX 978-542-6936
http://www.salem-ma.edu/graduate/msw4smft.htm

Simmons College
Graduate School of Social Work
51 Commonwealth Avenue
Boston, MA 02116
Joseph M. Regan, Dean

617-521-3900
FAX 617-521-3956
http://www.simmons.edu/programs/ssw/

Smith College
School for Social Work
Lilly Hall
Northampton, MA 01063
Anita Lightburn, Dean
413-585-7952
FAX 413-585-7994
http://www.smith.edu/ssw/

Springfield College
School of Social Work
263 Alden Street
Springfield, MA 01109-3797
Francine J. Vecchiolla, Dean
413-788-2401
FAX 413-788-2412
http://www.spfldcol.edu/

Michigan
Andrews University
Department of Social Work
Nethery Hall
Berrien Springs, MI 49104
Sharon Pittman, Chair
616-471-6135
FAX 616-471-3686
http://www.andrews.edu/academic/cas/social_work.html

Eastern Michigan University
Department of Social Work
King Hall, Room 411
Ypsilanti, MI 48197
Wanda Bracy, Department Head
Marti Bombyk, MSW Coordinator
734-487-0393
FAX 734-487-6832
http://www.emich.edu/public/swk/swkhome.htm

Grand Valley State University
School of Social Work
25 Commerce Street SW
Grand Rapids, MI 49503
Rodney Mulder, Dean
616-771-6550
FAX 616-771-6570
http://www.gvsu.edu/acad/flyers/swmsw.html

Michigan State University
School of Social Work
254 Baker Hall
East Lansing, MI 48824
Gary Anderson, Director
517-353-8632
FAX 517-353-3038
http://www.ssc.msu.edu/~sw/

University of Michigan
School of Social Work
1080 S. University
Ann Arbor, MI 48109-1106
Paula Allen-Meares, Dean
734-764-5340
FAX 734-764-9954
http://www.ssw.umich.edu/

Wayne State University
School of Social Work
4756 Cass Avenue
201 Thompson Home
Detroit, MI 48202
Leon W. Chestang, Dean
Margaret Brunhoser, Director
313-577-4400
FAX 313-577-8770
http://www.socialwork.wayne.edu/

Western Michigan University
School of Social Work
Kalamazoo, MI 49008-5034
Tracey Mabrey, Interim Director
616-387-3171
FAX 616-387-3183
http://www.wmich.edu/hhs/sw/

Minnesota
Augsburg College
Department of Social Work
2211 Riverside Avenue

Minneapolis, MN 55454
Glenda Dewberry Rooney, Director
612-330-1189
FAX 612-330-1493
http://www.augsburg.edu/msw/index.html

College of St. Catherine/University of St. Thomas
School of Social Work
Mail LOR 406
2115 Summit Avenue
St Paul, MN 55105
Barbara W. Shank, Dean
Angeline Barretta-Herman, Masters Program Director
651-962-5800
FAX 651-962-5819
http://department.stthomas.edu/grad/index.cfm

University of Minnesota–Duluth
Department of Social Work
220 Bohannon Hall
Duluth, MN 55812
Melanie Shepard, Director
218-726-8859
FAX 218-726-7185
http://www.d.umn.edu/~sw/

University of Minnesota–Twin Cities
School of Social Work
105 Peters Hall
1404 Gortner Avenue
St. Paul, MN 55108
Jean K. Quam, Director
612-625-1220
FAX 612-624-3744
http://ssw.che.umn.edu/

Mississippi

Jackson State University
School of Social Work
3825 Ridgewood Road
Suite 9
Jackson, MS 39211
Gwendolyn Prater, Dean
Harvey Dean, Acting Director
601-987-4388
FAX 601-364-2396
http://www.jsums.edu/

University of Southern Mississippi
School of Social Work
Box 5114
Hattiesburg, MS 39406
Earlie M. Washington, Director
601-266-4163
FAX 601-266-4165
http://www-dept.usm.edu/~socwork/

Missouri

Saint Louis University
School of Social Service
3550 Lindell Boulevard
St. Louis, MO 63103
Susan Tebb, Dean
314-977-2730
FAX 314-977-2731
http://www.slu.edu/colleges/SOCSVC/

Southwest Missouri State University
School of Social Work
Professional Building, Suite 200
901 S. National Avenue
Springfield, MO 65804
John Gunther, Director
417-836-6067
FAX 417-836-7688
http://www.smsu.edu/swk/

University of Missouri–Columbia
School of Social Work
729 Clark Hall
Columbia, MO 65211-4470
Charles D. Cowger, Director
573-884-1425
FAX 573-882-8926
http://web.missouri.edu/~sswmain/

Washington University
George Warren Brown School of Social Work
One Brookings Drive

Campus Box 1196
St. Louis, MO 63130-4899
Shanti K. Khinduka, Dean
314-935-6693
FAX 314-935-8511
http://gwbweb.wustl.edu/

Nebraska
University of Nebraska at Omaha
School of Social Work
Annex 40
60th and Dodge Streets
Omaha, NE 68182-0293
Sunny Andrews, Director
402-554-2793
FAX 402-554-3788
http://cid.unomaha.edu/~wwwpa/sw/swhome.html

Nevada
University of Nevada, Las Vegas
School of Social Work
4505 Maryland Parkway
Box 455032
Las Vegas, NV 89154-5032
Esther Langston, Director
702-895-4338
FAX 702-895-4079
http://www.nscee.edu/unlv/Colleges/Urban/

University of Nevada, Reno
School of Social Work
Business Building, Room 523
Mail Stop 090
Reno, NV 89557-0068
Dean Pierce, Director
Susan Kerr Chandler, Coordinator
775-784-6542
FAX 775-784-4573
http://www.unr.edu/hcs/ssw/index.html

New Hampshire
University of New Hampshire
Department of Social Work
Murkland Hall
15 Library Way
Durham, NH 03824-3596
Robert E. Jolley, Chair
Jerry Marx, MSW Program Coordinator
603-862-1799
FAX 603-862-4374
http://www.unh.edu/social-work/index.html

New Jersey
Kean University
Department of Social Work
Master of Social Work Program
1000 Morris Avenue
Hutchinson Hall, Room 305
Union, NJ 07083-7131
Carol Williams, Director
908-527-2634
FAX 908-289-5633
http://www.kean.edu/

Rutgers–The State University of New Jersey
School of Social Work
536 George Street
New Brunswick, NJ 08901-1167
Mary Edna Davidson, Dean
732-932-7253
FAX 732-932-8915
http://www.rutgers.edu/

Branch

Rutgers–The State University of New Jersey
School of Social Work
Camden Campus
327 Cooper Street
Camden, NJ 08102
Mary Edna Davidson, Dean
Ann Abbott, Associate Dean
609-225-6346
FAX 609-225-6155
http://camden-www.rutgers.edu/

Rutgers–The State University of New Jersey
School of Social Work
707 Hill Hall
Newark, NJ 07102
Mary Edna Davidson, Dean
Barbara Stoker, Assistant Dean
201-648-5092
FAX 201-648-1423
http://rutgers-newark.rutgers.edu/

New Mexico

New Mexico Highlands University
School of Social Work
Las Vegas, NM 87701
Alfredo A. Garcia, Dean
505-454-3563
FAX 505-454-3290
http://www.nmhu.edu/academics/schsocwork/

New Mexico State University
School of Social Work
P.O, Box 30001, MSC 3SW
Las Cruces, NM 88003-8001
Yosikazu DeRoos, Director
505-646-2143
FAX 505-646-4116
http://www.nmsu.edu/~socwork/depthom.html

New York

Adelphi University
School of Social Work
South Avenue
Garden City, NY 11530
Roger Levin, Acting Dean
516-877-4354
FAX 516-877-4392
http://www.adelphi.edu/socialwork/

Columbia University
School of Social Work
622 W. 113th Street
New York, NY 10025
Ronald A. Feldman, Dean
212-854-5189
FAX 212-854-4585
http://www.columbia.edu/cu/ssw/

Fordham University
Graduate School of Social Service
113 W. 60th Street
Lincoln Center Campus
New York, NY 10023-7479
Mary Ann Quaranta, Dean
212-636-6616
FAX 212-636-7876
http://www.columbia.edu/cu/ssw/

Hunter College of the City University of New York
School of Social Work
129 E. 79th Street
New York, NY 10021
Bogart Leashore, Dean
212-452-7085
FAX 212-452-7150
http://www.hunter.cuny.edu/socwork/

New York University
Shirley M. Ehrenkranz School of Social Work
One Washington Square North
New York, NY 10003
Thomas M. Meenaghan, Dean
212-998-5959
FAX 212-995-4172
http://www.nyu.edu/socialwork/

Roberts Wesleyan College
Master of Social Work Program
2301 Westside Drive
Rochester, NY 14624-1997
William R. Descoteaux, Director
716-594-6410
FAX 716-594-6480
http://www.rwc.edu/academic/social_w_s/index.htm

State University of New York at Stony Brook
School of Social Welfare
Health Sciences Center
Level 2, Room 093
Stony Brook, NY 11794-8231
Frances L. Brisbane, Dean

516-444-2139
FAX 516-444-8908
http://www.uhmc.sunysb.edu/socwelf/

State University of New York, University at Albany
School of Social Welfare
135 Western Avenue
Albany, NY 12222
Katharine Briar-Lawson, Dean
518-442-5324
FAX 518-442-5380
http://www.albany.edu/ssw/index.html

State University of New York, University at Buffalo
School of Social Work
359 Baldy Hall
Box 601050
Buffalo, NY 14260-1050
Lawrence Shulman, Dean
716-645-3381
FAX 716-645-3883
http://www.albany.edu/ssw/index.html

Syracuse University
School of Social Work
Sims Hall
Syracuse, NY 13244-1230
William L. Pollard, Dean
315-443-5550
FAX 315-443-5576
http://www.social.syr.edu/

Yeshiva University
Wurzweiler School of Social Work
Belfer Hall
2495 Amsterdam Avenue
New York, NY 10033
Sheldon R. Gelman, Dean
212-960-0820
FAX 212-960-0822
http://www.yu.edu/wurzweiler/

North Carolina

East Carolina University
School of Social Work and Criminal Justice Studies
Ragsdale Building, Room 134
Greenville, NC 27858-4353
Gary R. Lowe, Dean
252-328-4208
FAX 252-328-4196
http://www.ecu.edu/

University of North Carolina at Chapel Hill
School of Social Work
Tate-Turner-Kuralt Building, CB 3550
301 Pittsboro Street
Chapel Hill, NC 27599-3550
Richard L. Edwards, Dean
919-962-1225
FAX 919-962-0890
http://ssw.unc.edu/

North Dakota

University of North Dakota
Department of Social Work
Gillette Hall
Box 7135
Grand Forks, ND 58202-7135
G. Michael Jacobsen, Chairperson
701-777-2669
FAX 701-777-4257
http://www.und.nodak.edu/

Ohio

Case Western Reserve University
Mandel School of Applied Social Sciences
10900 Euclid Avenue
Cleveland, OH 44106-7164
Darlyne Bailey, Dean
216-368-2270
FAX 216-368-2850
http://msass.cwru.edu/

Cleveland State University[1]
Joint Master of Social Work Program
1983 E 24th Street
Cleveland, OH 44115
Maggie Jackson, Associate Director
216-687-4599
FAX 216-687-5590
http://www.ims.csuohio.edu/swk/swk_grad.html

Ohio State University
College of Social Work
300 Stillman Hall
1947 College Road
Columbus, OH 43210-1162
Tony Tripodi, Dean
Stanley Blostein, Director
614-292-5300
FAX 614-292-6940
http://www.csw.ohio-state.edu/

University of Akron[1]
School of Social Work
Joint MSW Program
Polsky Building, Room 411
Akron, OH 44325-8001
Virginia Fitch, Director
330-972-5739
FAX 330972-5739
http://www.ims.csuohio.edu/swk/swk_grad.html

University of Cincinnati
School of Social Work
P.O. Box 210108
Cincinnati, OH 45220
Philip Jackson, Director
513-556-4615
FAX 513-556-2077
http://www.uc.edu/socialwork/

Oklahoma

University of Oklahoma
School of Social Work
1005 Jenkins Avenue
Norman, OK 73019
Julia M. Norlin, Director
405-325-2821
FAX 405-325-7072
http://www.ou.edu/socialwork/

Oregon

Portland State University
Graduate School of Social Work
P.O. Box 751
Portland, OR 97207-0751
James H. Ward, Dean
503-725-4712
FAX 503-725-5545
http://www.ssw.pdx.edu/

Pennsylvania

Bryn Mawr College
Graduate School of Social Work and Social Research
300 Airdale Road
Bryn Mawr, PA 19010-1697
Ruth W. Mayden, Dean
610-520-2603
FAX 610-520-2613
http://www.brynmawr.edu/gsswsr/

Marywood University
School of Social Work
2300 Adams Avenue
Scranton, PA 18509-1598
William H. Simpson Whitaker, Dean
570-348-6282
FAX 570-961-4742
http://www.marywood.edu/goals.htm

Temple University
School of Social Administration
1301 Cecil B. Moore Avenue
Ritter Hall Annex, Room 555
Philadelphia, PA 19122
Curtis A. Leonard, Dean
Donna Chavers, Director
215-204-8623
FAX 215-204-9606
http://www.temple.edu/socialwork/

University of Pennsylvania
School of Social Work
3701 Locust Walk
Philadelphia, PA 19104-6214
Ira M. Schwartz, Dean
215-898-5511
FAX 215-573-2099
http://www.ssw.upenn.edu

University of Pittsburgh
School of Social Work
2117 Cathedral of Learning
Pittsburgh, PA 15260
David E. Epperson, Dean
412-624-6304
FAX 412-624-6323
http://www.pitt.edu/~pittssw/

Widener University
Center for Social Work Education
One University Place
Chester, PA 19013
Paula T. Silver, Director
610-499-1153
FAX 610-499-4617
http://muse.widener.edu/SocialWork/

Puerto Rico

University of Puerto Rico, Rio Piedras Campus
Beatriz Lassalle Graduate School of Social Work
P.O. Box 23345
San Juan, PR 00931-3345
Victor I. Garcia Toro, Director
787-763-3725
FAX 787-763-3725
http://www.upr.edu/

Rhode Island

Rhode Island College
School of Social Work
600 Mount Pleasant Drive
Providence, RI 02908
George D. Metrey, Dean
E. Belle Evans, Chair
401-456-8042
FAX 401-456-8620
http://www.ric.edu/socwk/

South Carolina

University of South Carolina
College of Social Work
Columbia, SC 29208
Frank B. Raymond III, Dean
803-777-5291
FAX 803-777-3498
http://www.sc.edu/cosw/

Tennessee

University of Tennessee
College of Social Work
109 Henson Hall
Knoxville, TN 37996-3333
Karen M. Sowers, Dean
423-974-3176
FAX 423-974-4803
http://www.csw.utk.edu/

Branches

University of Tennessee, Knoxville
114 Henson Hall
Knoxville, TN 37996-333
Judith Fiene, Associate Dean
423-974-9953
FAX 423-974-4803

University of Tennessee, Memphis
822 Beale Street
Room 220
Memphis, TN 38163
Hugh Vaughn, Acting Associate Dean
901-448-4463
FAX 901-448-4850

University of Tennessee, Nashville
1720 West End Avenue
Room 230

Nashville, TN 37203
William Bell, Associate Dean
615-329-1212
FAX 615-329-1267

Texas

Our Lady of the Lake University
Worden School of Social Service
411 S.W. 24th Street
San Antonio, TX 78207-4689
Carl M. Zimmer, Dean
210-434-3969
FAX 210-431-4028
http://www.ollusa.edu/academic/worden/worden.htm

University of Houston
Graduate School of Social Work
Houston, TX 77204-4492
Ira Colby, Dean
Michelle Sampson, Director
713-743-8085
FAX 713-743-3267
http://www.sw.uh.edu/

University of Texas at Arlington
School of Social Work
Box 19129
Arlington, TX 76019
Santos H. Hernandez, Dean
817-272-3181
FAX 817-272-5229
http://www2.uta.edu/ssw/

University of Texas at Austin
School of Social Work
1925 San Jacinto Boulevard
Austin, TX 78712
Barbara W. White, Dean
512-471-1937
FAX 512-471-7268
http://www.utexas.edu/depts/sswork/

Utah

Brigham Young University
School of Social Work
221 Knight Mangum Building
P.O. Box 24472
Provo, UT 84602-4472
Kyle L. Pehrson, Director
801-378-3282
FAX 801-378-4049
http://fhss.byu.edu/socwork/

University of Utah
Graduate School of Social Work
395 S. 1500 E.
Room 111
Salt Lake City, UT 84112-0260
Kay Dea, Dean
801-581-6192
FAX 801-585-3219
http://www.socwk.utah.edu/

Vermont

University of Vermont
Department of Social Work
228 Waterman Building
Burlington, VT 05405
Gale Burford, Director
Marty Dewees, Interim MSW Coordinator
802-656-8800
FAX 802-656-8565
http://www.uvm.edu/~socwork/index.html

Virginia

Norfolk State University
Ethelyn R. Strong School of Social Work
2401 Corprew Avenue
Norfolk, VA 23504
Joseph Dancy, Jr., Interim Dean
757-823-8668
FAX 757-823-2556
http://www.nsu.edu/Academics/social/socworkie.htm

Radford University
School of Social Work
Box 6958
Radford, VA 24142

Marilyn A. Rigby, Interim Director
Jackie Parker, Coordinator
540-831-5266
FAX 540-831-6629
http://www.runet.edu/~sowk-web/

Virginia Commonwealth University
School of Social Work
1001 W. Franklin Street
P.O. Box 842027
Richmond, VA 23284-2027
Frank R. Baskind, Dean
Marcia P. Harrison, Director
804-828-1030
FAX 804-828-7541
http://www.vcu.edu/slwweb/index.htm

Washington

Eastern Washington University
Inland Empire School of Social Work and Human Services
526 5th Street
Cheney, WA 99004-2431
Michael L. Frumkin, Dean
509-359-6482
FAX 509-359-6475
http://www.class.ewu.edu/SW/homepage.html

University of Washington
School of Social Work
4101 15th Avenue NE
Seattle, WA 98195-6299
Nancy R. Hooyman, Dean
206-685-1662
FAX 206-543-1228
http://depts.washington.edu/sswweb/

Walla Walla College
Graduate School of Social Work
204 S. College Avenue
College Place, WA 99324-1198
Standley L. Gellineau, Director
509-527-2590
FAX 509-527-2253
http://www.wwc.edu/

West Virginia

West Virginia University
School of Social Work and Public Administration
Division of Social Work
P.O. Box 6830
Morgantown, WV 26506-6830
Barry L. Locke, Director
304-293-3501
FAX 304-293-5936
http://www.wvu.edu/~socialwk/

Wisconsin

University of Wisconsin–Madison
School of Social Work
1350 University Avenue
Madison, WI 53706-1510
Joan Robertson, Director
608-262-3561
FAX 608-263-3836
http://polyglot.lss.wisc.edu/socwork/intro.html

University of Wisconsin–Milwaukee
School of Social Welfare
P.O. Box 786
Milwaukee, WI 53201
James A. Blackburn, Dean
414-229-4400
FAX 414-229-5311
http://www.uwm.edu/Dept/SSW/

[1] Collaborative program—Cleveland State University and University of Akron

Appendix B

Master of Social Work Programs in Candidacy by the Council on Social Work Education

The material in this Appendix is reprinted with permission of the Council on Social Work Education. The information is current as of September 1999.

Note: New programs working toward accreditation are required to qualify for candidacy. Candidacy, a pre-accreditation status, attests to the public and to prospective students that the program of social work has shown evidence of sound planning and of having the resources to implement its plans, has indicated its intent to work toward accreditation, and appears to have the potential to attain this goal. Subsequent to candidacy status, a program of social work is eligible to apply for initial accreditation after it has graduated students or if it will graduate students within the academic year in which the program presented was implemented fully. Students receiving a degree from a program in candidacy status receive full accreditation of that degree upon the program's successful and uninterrupted completion of candidacy and initial accreditation only if that degree was earned under the curriculum that receives initial accreditation.

California

California State University, Los Angeles
Department of Social Work
5151 State University Drive
Los Angeles, CA 90008
E. Frederick Anderson, Director
213-343-4680
FAX 213-343-5009
http://www.calstatela.edu/

Georgia

Georgia State University
Department of Social Work
College of Health Sciences
University Plaza
Atlanta, GA 30303-3083
James L. Wolk, Chair
404-651-3526
FAX 404-651-1863
http://www.gsu.edu

Savannah State University
Master's Department of Social Work
College of Liberal Arts and Social Sciences
P.O. Box 20553
Savannah, GA 31404
Beverly A. Watkins, Chair
912-356-2410
FAX 912-356-2458
http://www.savstate.edu/

Illinois

Southern Illinois University at Edwardsville
Department of Social Work
College of Arts and Sciences
Peck Building, Room 1231
Edwardsville, IL 62026-1455
Thomas Regulus, Chair
618-650-5758
FAX 618-650-3509
http://www.siue.edu/SOCIAL/

Iowa

St. Ambrose University
School of Social Work
518 W. Locust Street
Davenport, IA 52803
Kathylene Siska, Director
319-333-6379
FAX 319-333-6097
http://www.sau.edu/academic/MSW/MSWWEB.htm

Kansas

Newman University
Graduate School of Social Work
3100 McCormick Avenue
Wichita, KS 67213-2097
Vimala Pillari, Director
316-942-4291
FAX 316-942-4483
http://www.ksnewman.edu/

Wichita State University
Social Work Department
Hugo Wall School of Urban and Public Affairs
Box 135
1845 Fairmount
Wichita, KS 67260-0135
Cathleen A. Lewandowski, Director
316-978-7250
FAX 316-978-3626
http://www.wichita.edu/

Kentucky

Spalding University
Department of Social Work
851 S. Fourth Street
Louisville, KY 40203-2115
Jillian Johnson, Chair
502-585-9911
FAX 502-585-7159
http://www.spalding.edu/graduate/socwrk/docmsw.htm

Grambling State University
School of Social Work
P.O. Box 907
Grambling, LA 71245
Birdex Copeland Jr., Dean
318-274-3305
FAX 318-274-3254

Missouri

University of Missouri–St. Louis
Department of Social Work
College of Arts and Sciences
8001 Natural Bridge Road
St. Louis, MO 63121-4499
Joan Hashimi, Chair
314-516-6385
FAX 314-516-5816
http://www.umsl.edu/~socialwk/

New Jersey

Monmouth University
Social Work Department
Norwood and Cedar Avenue
West Long Branch, NJ 07764-1898
Mark E. Rodgers, Chair
732-571-3543
FAX 732-263-5217
http://www.monmouth.edu/~swork/

North Carolina

University of North Carolina Greensboro/North Carolina A & T State University
Joint Masters Program
Gibbs Social Science Building
1601 E. Market Street
Greensboro, NC 27411-0002
Sarah V. Kirk, Director
336-334-7894
FAX 336-334-7197
http://www.uncg.edu/swk/joint_msw.htm

Ohio

Ohio University
Department of Social Work
531 Morton Hall
Athens, OH 45701-2949
Carolyn Tice, MSW Coordinator
740-593-1291
FAX 740-593-0427
http://www-as.phy.ohiou.edu/Departments/SocWrk/

Pennsylvania

West Chester University
Department of Graduate Social Work
McCoy Center South Campus
West Chester, PA 19383
Larry Ortiz, Director
610-436-2664
FAX 610-436-2135
http://www.wcupa.edu/

Puerto Rico

Universidad Interamericana de Puerto Rico, Recinto de Metropolitano
Graduate Social Work Program
P.O. Box 191293
San Juan, PR 00919-1293
Carmen Escoda Lastra, Director
787-250-1912 ext. 2358/2272
FAX 787-250-6843

Texas

Baylor University
School of Social Work
P.O. Box 97326
Waco, TX 76798-7326
Preston Dyer, Chair
Diana Garland, Director
254-710-6230
FAX 254-710-1175
http://www.baylor.edu/

Southwest Texas State University
Department of Social Work
Walter Richter Institute of Social
Work Research
601 University Drive
San Marcos, TX 78666-4616
J. Karen Brown, Chair
Nancy Feyl Chavkin, Director
512-245-8833
FAX 512-245-8097
http://www.health.swt.edu/SOWK/
SOWK.html

Stephen F. Austin State University
Master of Social Work Program
School of Social Work
P.O. Box 6104
SFA Station
Nacogdoches, TX 75962-6104
Michael R. Daley, Director
409-468-4020
FAX 409-468-7201
http://www.sfasu.edu/aas/socwk/

University of Texas–Pan American
Department of Social Work
1201 W. University Drive
Edinburg, TX 78539-2999
Librado de Hoyos, Director
956-381-3575
FAX 956-381-3516
http://www.panam.edu/

Wyoming

University of Wyoming
Department of Social Work
Box 3632
Laramie, WY 82071
Pat Conway, Chair
307-766-6112
FAX 307-766-6839
http://august.uwyo.edu/
SocialWork/sowk.htm

Appendix C

In Their Own Words: Responses to a Survey of Master of Social Work Programs

In an effort to provide the latest information from the schools themselves, a survey was devised and distributed to all the social work graduate programs either accredited or in candidacy for accreditation by the Council on Social Work Education at the time of the survey. Sixty-seven of the programs returned a completed survey.

The survey sought information in five major areas: contact information, unique aspects of each program, student organizations, tips to applicants about unique factors the school looks for in applicants, and tips on common mistakes made by applicants. Most schools responded to every item, but a few chose not to respond to some items.

Item I (contact information) of the survey had as its goal to provide applicants with as many current means of contacting and obtaining information from each school as possible. It asked the name of a contact person, mailing address, telephone and fax numbers, as well as e-mail and Web site addresses. Some of this information differs slightly from that provided in Appendix A and B. This is because the information in this section, in some cases, tells how to contact the admissions office directly, whereas that in Appendix A and B is the general contact information for the school.

Item II (unique aspects of the program) sought to learn how each school views itself as compared to other programs. What does it offer (academically or otherwise) that is different from what is available at other schools? The responses are insightful not only in the information they provide about specific programs (such as rural or international social work options) but also because they reveal a great deal about each school's philosophy.

Item III (student organizations) sought to learn about opportunities for student involvement. As noted elsewhere, extracurricular experiences can round out a graduate education nicely.

Item IV (tips for applicants) was intended to provide applicants with insight into each school's admission philosophy. It is interesting to note that each school seeks a match at two levels: (a) the general values of the profession of social work and (b) the program's specific values as reflected in its offerings.

Item V (common mistakes) sought to provide "words to the wise" about pitfalls to avoid in the application process. Some common themes emerged and the reader would be wise to read the comments of all the schools, whether or not she intends to apply to a given school.

As much as the need for brevity allows, each school's responses are included in this Appendix essentially as the school itself wrote them. As might be expected, each school sought to "put its best foot forward" in its responses. Therefore, the responses also offer insight into what each school sees as its best qualities. In short, the responses are those of the schools, not of the publisher or the author, and do not imply any endorsement of any school or program on the part of the publisher or the author. Nevertheless, the responses are assumed to be accurate in that they were given in a responsible fashion by the schools. Applicants should obtain further information from the schools themselves, as the information provided at the time of the survey may have changed.

The responding schools are listed alphabetically below. Elsewhere in this book, you may find all the schools listed by state location.

Andrews University, Department of Social Work, Nethery Hall, Berrien Springs, MI 49104-0038. Admissions Contact Person: Alice McIntyre. Phone: 616-471-6538 or 888-297-9280. Fax: 616-471-3686. E-Mail: mcintyre@andrews.edu. Web Site Address: http://www.andrews.edu/academic/cas/social_work.html

Unique aspects of the program: At Andrews University, the Christian perspective in social work comes to life. You will develop practical skills for really making a difference in the lives of hurting people and within broken communities. You will grow professionally while making friends for life. Graduates are prepared to work in interpersonal practice settings or in administration and development.

Student Organizations: Student Forum

Tips for Applicants: The prerequisites of the General GRE and a course in human biology most frequently hold people back. The sooner an applicant completes these two requirements, the more quickly he/she can be accepted in regular standing. While the GRE is a requirement, applicants should not be overly concerned about the score, since it is only a small component of the entire process.

Common Applicant Mistakes: Because of the way the University has set up the application process, various components of the application packet need to be returned to the correct office on campus. Take extra care to be sure that each item is mailed directly to the place the instructions indicate. This will speed up the application process significantly.

Augsburg College Department of Social Work, 2211 Riverside Avenue, Minneapolis, MN 55454. Phone: 612-330-1307. Fax: 612-330-1493. E-Mail: swkinfo@augsburg.edu. Web Site Address: http://www.augsburg.edu/msw/index.html

Unique aspects of the program: High level of diversity; located in the heart of Minneapolis. Two areas of specialization are Family Practice and Public Policy.

Student Organizations: MSW Student Forum

Tips for Applicants: Give examples of experience and service.

Barry University School of Social Work, 11300 N.E. 2nd Avenue, Miami Shores, FL 33161. Admissions Contact Person: Philip S. Mack, Director of Admissions. Phone: 305-899-3900 or 800-756-6000, ext. 3900. Fax: 305-899-3934. E-Mail: pmack@mail.barry.edu. Web Site Address: http://www2.barry.edu/vpaa-ssw/default.htm

Unique aspects of the program: The MSW program is known for its rich tradition of training graduates for clinical social work practice. Areas of specialization include Children and Families and Health and Mental Health. Students may study full time or part time. Applicants who have a BSW degree received within the last five years may qualify for enrollment into the Advanced Standing program and graduate with the MSW degree in nine months.

Student Organizations: Student Government

Tips for Applicants: The School looks for students who have a GPA of 3.0 or better in their last two years (60 credits) of college. Each individual application is reviewed and assessed based on the quality of each applicant's academic performance, work or volunteer experience, personal written statement, and references.

Common Applicant Mistakes: Applicants often do not submit transcripts from each college attended, thereby delaying the review process.

Brigham Young University, School of Social Work, 221 Knight Mangum Building, P.O. Box 24472, Provo, UT 84602-4472. Admissions Contact Person: Lisa Willey, Graduate Secretary. Phone: 801-378-3282. Fax: 801-378-4049. E-Mail: socialwork@byu.edu. Web Site Address: http://fhss.byu.edu/socwork/

Unique aspects of the program: Five-semester program. Comprehensive multidiscipline clinic for helping professionals with up-to-date taping facility available.

Student Organizations: Student Branch of the Utah Chapter of the National Association of Social Workers

Tips for Applicants: The School seeks applicants who are committed to the values of the social work profession.

Common Applicant Mistakes: Not following application directions; poorly written essay.

Bryn Mawr College Graduate School of Social Work and Social Research, 300 Airdale Road, Bryn Mawr, PA 19010. Admissions Contact Person: Nancy J. Kirby, Director of Admissions. Phone: 610-520-2601. Fax: 610-520-2655. E-Mail: swadmiss@brynmawr.edu. Web Site Address: http://www.brynmawr.edu

Unique aspects of the program: Option to complete a Master's degree in Law and Social Policy (MLSP) either as a joint degree program with the Master of Social Service (MSS) or as a post master's degree. Student representation on all committees, including Admissions, Curriculum, Field Instruction, Faculty Search, Evaluation of Student Performance. Extensive career development program. Alumnae/i mentors. Diverse student population, including traditional age college graduates, those with significant human service experience, and those making career changes.

Student Organizations: Student Association; National Association of Black Social Workers Chapter; student organized support groups in areas of interest such as social action; spirituality; gay, lesbian, and transgendered persons.

Tips for Applicants: Bryn Mawr looks for self-awareness; flexibility; related human service experience through internships, employment, and/or volunteer work; strong writing skills; demonstrated ability to handle demanding academic curriculum. An interview is required of all applicants.

Common Applicant Mistakes: Frequent mistakes include failure to: thoughtfully compose and edit the essay; file financial aid forms in a timely manner; give careful thought to selection of references.

California State University, Sacramento Division of Social Work, Tahoe Hall, 6000 J Street, Sacramento, CA 95819-6090. Admissions Contact Person: Dr. Joan Dworkin. Phone: 916-278-6943. Fax: 916-278-7167

Unique aspects of the program: We offer an advanced generalist concentration that prepares in the breadth and depth of clinical and social change practice in multicultural contexts.

Student Organizations: Graduate Social Work Student Association

Comments: The School seeks evidence of (1) commitment to empowerment of pluralistic communities, agencies, neighborhoods, and (2) experience in use of self in multicultural social work contexts.

Common Applicant Mistakes: (1) Personal statements narrowly emphasizing clinical or community-oriented practice and not advanced generalist practice, (2) GPAs lower than 2.7 for the last 60 credit hours of undergraduate work.

California State University, San Bernardino Department of Social Work, 5500 University Parkway, San Bernardino, CA 92407-2397. Admissions Contact Person: Dr. Nancy Mary. Phone: 909-880-5501. Fax: 909-880-7029. E-Mail: nmary@csusb.edu. Web Site Address: http://ssbs.csusb.edu/social_work/

Unique aspects of the program: We have three specializations: Mental Health; Children, Youth, and Families; and Macro Practice. We are situated on the attractive CSUSB campus at the foot of the San Bernardino Mountains, 60 miles east of Los Angeles. We have an enthusiastic faculty and a diverse student body with strong ties to the local area. For most of the year, the sun is shining and the temperature is pleasantly warm.

Student Organizations: We have the Social Work Student Association, which organizes events and a separate graduation for MSW students. We also have a Title IV-E Alumni Association for students who were in the Child Welfare stipend program while pursuing their MSWs.

Tips for Applicants: As well as a GPA of 3.0 or above, we look for a social work background, a personal statement that reflects a mature understanding of social work, and references that address an applicant's ability to relate well to clients, problem solve, and follow through on work assignments.

Common Applicant Mistakes: The personal statement is not organized and hasn't been proofread.

California State University, Stanislaus Department of Social Work, 801 West Monte Vista Avenue, Turlock, CA 95382. Admissions Contact Per-

son: Ellen Dunbar, Ph.D., Director of MSW Program. Phone: 209-667-3091. Fax: 209-667-3869. Web Site Address: http://www.csustan.edu/Social_Work/index.htm

Unique aspects of the program: This is a small program of quality. There is an outstanding teaching faculty. The curriculum focus is on integrative practice, collaboration, diversity, and community. The curriculum stresses strengths perspective and maintains that work with individuals and with community requires skills that are compatible. Research for practice is emphasized. Both rural and urban practicum sites are available.

Student Organizations: MSW Student Association

Common Applicant Mistakes: Applicants need to apply to the University for postbaccalaureate standing in addition to applying to our program. Failure to do either of these results in incomplete files, which cannot be reviewed for admission.

Case Western Reserve University, Mandel School of Applied Social Sciences, 10900 Euclid Avenue, Cleveland, OH 44106-7164. Admissions Contact Person: Ann E. Toomey. Phone: 216-368-2280 or 800-863-6772. Fax: 216-368-5065. E-Mail: prp5@po.cwru.edu. Web Site Address: http://msass.cwru.edu

Unique aspects of the program: The Mandel School is a top-ranked graduate school of social work that offers master's, doctoral, and joint degrees. The School is one of the few schools of social work that offer courses in international social work.

Student Organizations: LINK (Local International Konnections); Intensive Weekend Student Caucus; African-American Student Association; Student Coordinating Board; Non-Traditional Student Caucus

Clark Atlanta University School of Social Work, 223 James P. Brawley Drive, S.W., Atlanta, GA 30314-4391. Admissions Contact Person: Anne Fields-Ford, Ph.D. Phone: 404-880-8553. Fax: 404-880-6434. Web Site Address: http://www.cau.edu/

Unique aspects of the program: The School has a clinical concentration. There are two areas of specialization: Health/Mental Health and Child and Family. The Child and Family has a sub-specialization in School Social Work.

Student Organizations: CAU School of Social Work Student Association

Tips for Applicants: (1) A baccalaureate degree that reflects a broad liberal arts base, (2) openness, (3) maturity, (4) capacity for empathy, (5) psychologically minded, (6) interest in working with people in a professional helping role.

Common Applicant Mistakes: Some autobiographical statements are too short and do not reflect the applicants' experience and reasons for choosing social work as a profession.

Cleveland State University/University of Akron Joint MSW Program, Cleveland State University, 1983 E. 24th Street, Cleveland, OH 44115. Admissions Contact Person: Dr. Maggie Jackson, Director. Phone: 216-687-4599. Fax: 216-687-5590. E-Mail: Mag.Jackson@csuohio.edu. Web Site Address: http://www.ims.csuohio.edu/swk/swk_grad.html

Unique aspects of the program: This is a joint Master of Social Work Program. Classes are held via interactive television between the two universities. Faculty are from both universities. This program is based on Generalist Practice with concentrations in Micro (direct) and Macro Practice.

Student Organizations: MSW Student Organization

Tips for Applicants: Must have a background in the social and behavioral sciences. Social work experiences are not required, but may enhance the application. Both paid and volunteer experiences are considered.

Common Applicant Mistakes: The GRE is required of prospective students who graduated more than six years previous to the application date and/or have an undergraduate GPA below 2.75. These scores must be in the fiftieth percentile and received prior to the application deadline of March 15.

College of St. Catherine/University of St. Thomas School of Social Work, 2115 Summit Avenue, Mail #LOR406, St. Paul, MN 55105-1096. Admissions Contact Person: Angeline Barretta-Herman, Ph.D., MSW Program Coordinator. Phone: 651-962-5804. Fax: 651-962-5819. E-Mail: a9barrettahe@stthomas.edu. Web Site Address: http://www.stthomas.edu/www/socwork_http/index.html

Unique aspects of the program: The MSW prepares social work practitioners for clinical social work practice and leadership with a focus on direct clinical services or clinical supervision and program management. The program features small classes, personal attention, excellent teaching faculty with extensive practice experience, and a strong field program with placements in over ninety agencies.

The program is offered jointly by the College of St. Catherine and the University of St. Thomas. Classes are offered on both campuses late afternoons and evenings to accommodate working students. Selected classes are offered early afternoons, weekends, and summers. Students with a BSW from a CSWE accredited program are eligible for advanced standing. Otherwise, the MSW is a 60 credit program that can be completed full time in two years or in extended time in three or four years.

Faculty scholarship/research productivity rates are high and faculty are active in national, international, and professional organizations. A dual degree program in Theology has been established with the College of St. Catherine, Luther Seminary, and the St. Paul Seminary School of Divinity. The Supervision Institute offers training and consultation to practitioners and agencies in clinical supervision, supervision for licensure, and supports an active research program. A Spirituality Institute and a Group Work Institute are planned.

Student Organizations: Opportunities for student involvement include membership on each of the five curriculum committees, research assistantships, and membership on faculty/staff search committees. There is no MSW student organization at this time.

Tips for Applicants: Applicants with social service experience who have demonstrated their ability to establish relationships and work with diverse individuals, families, and small groups dealing with multiple challenges are strong candidates. Students have an average age of 33 with 5 to 6 years experience in the field. The age range is 24 to 64. Students with language skills or international or social justice experience are particularly competitive. All applicants are required to have an undergraduate GPA of at least 3.0, although provisional acceptance is offered to otherwise well qualified applicants.

Common Applicant Mistakes: Writing a personal statement that is not sufficiently comprehensive and informative for the admissions committee to make an assessment of suitability and of writing skills. Submitting letters of reference that are not specific enough. The more specific recommenders are about the candidate's skills and abilities, particularly if they have observed or supervised the candidate's work with clients, the stronger the application.

Florida International University School of Social Work, 3000 N.E. 151st Street, North Miami, FL 33181. Admissions Contact Person: David T. Poole, Enrollment Services Coordinator. Phone: 305-919-5609. Fax: 305-919-5980. E-Mail: cupa@fiu.edu. Web Site Address: http://www.fiu.edu/~cupa/social-work.html

Unique aspects of the program: FIU/HRS Professional Development Center; FIU's Institute for Children and Families at Risk.

Student Organizations: Phi Alpha Honor Society

Florida State University School of Social Work, University Center C2501, Tallahassee, FL 32306-2570. Admissions Contact Person: Julie Iarussi, Special Assistant to the Dean. Phone: 850-644-4751 or 800-378-9550. Fax: 850-644-9750. E-Mail: grad@ssw.fsu.edu. Web Site Address: http://ssw.fsu.edu

Unique aspects of the program: The School offers degrees at the Bachelor's, Master's, and Doctoral levels. Dual degrees are offered in MSW/MPA, MSW/JD, and MSW/Ph.D. in Social Work. Two concentrations are offered within the MSW program: 1) Community Based Clinical and 2) Social Policy and Administration. Certificate programs are available in Aging Studies, Family Social Work, School Social Work, the Arts and Community Practice, and Traumatology.

Student Organizations: Phi Alpha National Social Work Honor Society; Association of Student Social Workers; Congress of Graduate Students

Tips for Applicants: The School looks for well-rounded, diverse individuals who possess excellent written and verbal skills, along with high academic merit and job and volunteer experience.

Common Applicant Mistakes: Applicants should take care to fill out all sections of the application. Applicants are encouraged to have all transcripts, recommendations, and GRE scores forwarded to the School in a timely manner. Applications cannot be processed if all pieces are not received. A typical problem is that students wait too long to take the GRE and/or the TOEFL. These should be taken as soon as possible to ensure that scores are received quickly.

Gallaudet University, MSW Program, 800 Florida Avenue, NE, Washington, DC 20002-3695. Admissions Contact Person: Janet L. Pray. Phone: 202-651-5160. Fax: 202-651-5817. Web Site Address: http://www.gallaudet.edu/~swweb/

Unique aspects of the program: We are the only graduate program in social work in the world with the exclusive mission of preparing deaf, hard of hearing, and hearing social workers for social work practice with deaf and hard of hearing people. Students are prepared for work with individuals, families, groups, organizations, and communities.

Student Organizations: Graduate Student Association

Tips for Applicants: Prior knowledge of sign language is a definite plus. We are also interested in people interested in gerontology, particularly in the area of late onset hearing loss.

Common Applicant Mistakes: Choosing references who do not submit their recommendations within a reasonable period of time; applications that do not include clear statements regarding selection of social work as a career, particularly social work with deaf and hard of hearing people; spelling and typographical errors on the application.

Hunter College School of Social Work, 129 East 79th Street, New York, NY 10021. Admissions Contact Person: Yvonne Purnomo. Phone: 212-452-7005. Fax: 212-452-7140. E-Mail: ypurnomo@hejira.hunter.cuny.edu. Web Site Address: http://www.hunter.cuny.edu/socwork

Unique aspects of the program: Hunter is the only public graduate school of social work in New York City and one of the most selective in the nation (an average 40% acceptance rate). The student body is diverse, and the School's graduates are leaders in creative and innovative practice. The School is housed in its own ten-floor, multimillion-dollar building constructed for it by the Lois and Samuel Silberman Fund. The MSW curriculum is designed for agency-based practice using all of the four major practice methods (casework, groupwork, community organization, and administration).

Student Organizations: Board of Student Representatives and various alliances including: Black Students Alliance, Hispanic Alliance, Asian Alliance, Arts Alliance, Feminist Alliance, Jewish Student Alliance, Gay and Lesbian Alliance, Parents Alliance, Students with Disabilities Alliance, AIDS Advocacy Alliance, Clinical Alliance, Cyclists Alliance, and a Student Chapter of the National Association of Black Social Workers.

Tips for Applicants: Strong liberal arts background, voluntary or paid experience in social work settings, and a commitment to diverse and vulnerable populations.

Indiana University Northwest, Division of Social Work, 3400 Broadway, Gary, IN 46408. Admissions Contact Person: Fran Goldie. Phone: 219-980-7111. Fax: 219-981-4264. E-Mail: fgoldie@iunhawl.iun.indiana.edu. Web Site Address: http://www.iun.indiana.edu/socialwk/

Unique aspects of the program: We offer both a three-year and a four-year part-time program with a concentration in either interpersonal or macro practice. The program is designed for working professionals. Advanced standing is possible for graduates of CSWE-accredited BSW programs. We do not offer a full-time program.

Student Organizations: Phi Alpha Honor Society

Tips for Applicants: We look for applicants who demonstrate a commitment to social and economic justice and are committed to the values of the social work profession.

Common Applicant Mistakes: The most common mistake is emphasizing a narrow interest in the field of social work that does not reflect an appreciation for the values of our profession. A second common error is turning in a narrative that contains grammatical, spelling, or other major writing mistakes.

Kean University Master of Social Work Program, J-309L, 1000 Morris Avenue, Union, NJ 07083. Admissions Contact Person: Bettie Rogers, MSW, LSW, Director of Admissions. Phone: 908-527-2835/3290. Fax: 908-289-5633. E-Mail: brogers@turbo.Kean.edu. Web Site Address: http://turbo.Kean.edu/

Unique aspects of the program: Our concentration is Advanced Generalist wherein students obtain learning in theory and practice that enables them to work within various professional roles serving systems of all sizes. Our professional program prepares students and places graduates at the top of the competition in the job market. We offer a small student to faculty ratio, which affords interpersonal interaction and guidance. An advanced standing option is offered to qualified BSW applicants who can earn the MSW degree in one year. We provide a vast selection of community internship positions in New Jersey and New York. Tuition is low in comparison to other graduate institutions. The cost per semester for New Jersey residents is $2,963.20, and for out-of-state students is $3,655.70. Classes are held twice a week, on Wednesday evenings from 5:00 until 10:30 p.m., and on Fridays, 8:00 a.m. until 3:30 p.m. There are graduate assistantship opportunities available, and work-study is also a possibility to assist in financing the 2-year course of study.

Student Organizations: MSW Student Organization; Phi Alpha Honor Society

Tips for Applicants: Unique factors that we seek in the admissions process and in our students are their sincere interest in the profession, possessing the desire to assist and to work with populations-at-risk in terms of moving them toward self-sufficiency, and to quality of life situations, albeit medical, educational, social services. We look at professional involvement at all levels: employment, volunteer services, continuing education in the field, including and not limited to professional and personal deportment and experiences.

Common Applicant Mistakes: Applicants fail to follow the "written" directions as stated in the application. This occurs often with the personal statement. Also, submitted applications make a better impression on the readers when typed. Applicants take it for granted that their hand-writing is legible.

Loyola University Chicago, School of Social Work, 820 N. Michigan Avenue, Chicago, IL 60611. Admissions Contact Person: Jude Gonzales, Admissions Advisor. Phone: 312-915-7011. Fax: 312-915-7645. E-Mail: MSW_LUC!@luc.edu. Web Site Address: http://www.luc.edu/schools/socialwork/

Unique aspects of the program: Loyola's clinical social work focus prepares students to practice in mental health, school social work, child welfare, family and elderly services, substance abuse, employee assistance, and counseling of individuals, families, and small groups. Loyola offers two dual degree programs: MSW/JD and MSW/M.Div.

Student Organizations: Graduate Student Association (GSA), Minority Alumni Recruitment Committee (MARC)

Tips for Applicants: Loyola looks favorably on a well-rounded undergraduate preparation, preferably in the liberal arts. At least one of the letters of recommendation should be from a social service agency where the applicant has worked, either paid or volunteer. Applicants should be sure to answer all of the bulleted points in the personal statement instructions.

Common Applicant Mistakes: Sending in the application before it is complete; getting all letters of recommendation from one type of source; making the personal statement too short, not answering the points outlined in the instructions.

Marywood University School of Social Work, 2300 Adams Avenue, Scranton, PA 18509. Admissions Contact Person: Virginia Haskett, Director of Admissions. Phone: 800-548-4898 or 570-348-6282. Fax: 570-961-4742. E-Mail: vhaskett@ac.marywood.edu or ssw_adm@marywood.edu. Web Site Address: http://www.marywood.edu/goals.htm

Unique aspects of the program: Curriculum stresses versatility rather than specialization. Entering class forms a cohort and moves together through the program. Classes are small and all classes are available in the evening (Allentown Campus) and on Saturdays (Scranton Campus).

Student Organizations: Social Work Student Association

Tips for Applicants: A personal interview is scheduled with each applicant. The applicant should be ready to define learning goals for graduate work. An application essay is required that describes what the applicant has learned from formal education, work, and life experience.

Common Applicant Mistakes: Failing to recognize the difference between counseling or therapy and social work; defining a single, exclusive practice interest; supplying references from academic sources only.

Monmouth University Department of Social Work, 400 Cedar Avenue, West Long Branch, NJ 07764. Admissions Contact Person: Mary Jo Macro. Phone: 732-571-3543. Fax: 732-263-5217. E-Mail: rodgers@monmouth.edu. Web Site Address: http://www.monmouth.edu/~swork/

Unique aspects of the program: Our MSW program utilizes a strengths perspective, an empowerment approach, and focuses on families globally. We have two concentrations: (1) Services to Families and Children and (2) International Social Work/Community Development. Field placements in overseas international settings are possible.

Student Organizations: Social Work Society; Social Work Honor Society – Alpha Beta Chapter

Tips for Applicants: MSW applications are accepted through March 1. An interest in international social work is valued.

New Mexico State University School of Social Work, P.O. Box 30001, MSC 3SW, Las Cruces, NM 88003-8001. Admissions Contact Person: Barbara Chandler. Phone: 505-646-2143. Fax: 505-646-4116. E-Mail: bachand1@nmsu.edu. Web Site Address: http://www.nmsu.edu/~socwork/depthom.html

Unique aspects of the program: The concentration, Family-Centered Practice in Multicultural Settings, addresses the program's primary strength, the ability to focus on working with families while addressing issues of cultural diversity to best prepare our graduates for social work in the new millennium.

Student Organizations: Graduate Social Work Student Association (GSWSA)

Tips for Applicants: The School of Social Work at New Mexico State University seeks applicants who best fit with the goals of the MSW program and the values of the profession. It seeks a student population rich in diversity and committed to the support of families.

Common Applicant Mistakes: The applicant may fail to (a) apply to both the Graduate School and the MSW program, (b) read the application packet carefully and lose valuable time in the application process, (c) complete the undergraduate courses required by the School of Social Work before applying to the MSW program, and (d) insure that all materials needed by the School, in particular letters of reference, reach the program.

New York University, Shirley M. Ehrenkranz School of Social Work, One Washington Square North, New York, NY 10003-6654. Admissions Contact Person: Stuart A.Gitlin, Director of Admissions and Financial Aid. Phone: 212-998-5910. Fax: 212-995-4171. E-Mail: essw.admissions@nyu.edu. Web Site Address: http://www.nyu.edu/socialwork/

Unique aspects of the program: The School is one of the leading centers in professional training in direct social work practice. Graduates acquire the core knowledge and skills to work directly with individuals, families, and groups. This is our only major and we focus our energy within this model of practice.

Student Organizations: Graduate Student Association (GSA); African-American, Hispanic-American, Asian-American and Native-American Association (AHANA); Bisexual, Gay and Lesbian Student Association (BGLAD); PEER Support

Tips for Applicants: Provide us with examples of your people skills, especially, but not only, in a helping environment. As a direct practice school, if your grades are adequate, we are looking for experience involved with people. Do not neglect the fact that we are still social workers and concerned with aspects of social justice.

Common Applicant Mistakes: Read the directions on the application, especially for the essay. Respond to the questions and proofread. Make sure you are sending the right essay to the right school.

Newman University, Graduate School of Social Work, 3100 McCormick Avenue, Wichita, KS 67213. Admissions Contact Person: Vimala Pillari. Phone: 316-942-4291. Fax: 316-942-4483. E-Mail: pillariv@newmanu.edu. Web Site Address: http://www.ksnewman.edu

Unique aspects of the program: MSW graduate program with a Family-Centered concentration. We offer full-time and part-time programs, as well as an Advanced Standing program. We feature small classes with individualized attention and a nurturing learning environment with highly qualified faculty.

Student Organizations: Social Work Club

The Ohio State University, College of Social Work, 1947 College Road, Columbus, OH 43210. Admissions Contact Person: Sharon Schweitzer. Phone: 614-292-2972. Fax: 614-292-6940. Web Site Address: http://www.csw.ohio-state.edu

Unique aspects of the program:

- Faculty are readily accessible in addressing student questions outside the classroom
- A plethora of placements throughout the Columbus vicinity and 88 counties in Ohio
- The program offers a social administrative and clinical focus
- Students have autonomy in selecting elective courses that complement their prac-

tice scope
- The library allows access to other university libraries throughout Ohio
- There is an optional thesis requirement for completion of the MSW degree
- The College of Social Work library has over 40,000 volumes and subscribes to over 300 journals
- There is a 24-hour computing laboratory available to students

Student Organizations: Social Work Student Association; Alpha Delta MU—National Social Work Honor Society; Mwanafunzi—a student chapter of the National Association of Black Social Workers; Student and College Liaison Committee; students are represented on every standing committee of the College except the Promotion and Tenure Committee

Tips for Applicants: Applicants should indicate (1) a concise understanding of social work principles and values, (2) history of paid or volunteer experiences, and (3) their unique characteristics and personal and academic interests. Applicants may include a résumé to document experiences and goals.

Common Applicant Mistakes: Applicant does not thoroughly read the application instructions and adhere to the College deadlines that are different from those of the University. Applicant does not obtain appropriate recommendations. References should speak to an individual's ability to successfully complete a graduate program. Appropriate resources include professional as well as academic reviewers.

Portland State University, Graduate School of Social Work, P. O. Box 751 (for mailing), 527 SW Hall (mail not received at this address), Portland, OR 97207. Admissions Contact Person: Janet Putnam. Phone: 503-725-4712. Fax: 503-725-5545. E-Mail: putnamj@pdx.edu. Web Site Address: http://www.ssw.pdx.edu

Unique aspects of the program: The Graduate School of Social Work is nationally ranked/recognized and noted in *U.S. News & World Report* and provides the opportunity for advanced study in one of three areas: direct human services, community based practice, or social service program management. Areas of specialization include mental health, services to children, youth and their families, health care, services to the elderly, and homeless populations. The School also has a nationally recognized Research Institute for Human Services, which serves the region and national research interests.

Student Organizations: Organization of Graduate Students in Social Work (OGSSW); Lavender Forum; Students for Diversity

Tips for Applicants: The GSSW seeks applicants who are well qualified academically for graduate study and have a demonstrated commitment to the mission of social work. The School is also interested in students who bring diversity to the program through life experience, cultural background, or ethnicity.

Common Applicant Mistakes: Submitting an incomplete application; failure to prepare a personal statement that clearly expresses the applicant's values, beliefs, and personal philosophy and their relationship to the social work mission.

Roberts Wesleyan College, The Division of Social Work & Social Sciences, 2301 Westside Drive, Rochester, NY 14624. Admissions Contact Person: Jim Sheets. Phone: 716-594-6410. Fax: 716-594-6480. E-Mail: sheetsj@roberts.edu. Web Site Address: http://www.rwc.edu/academic/social_w_s/index.htm

Unique aspects of the program: The program has three concentrations: Child/Family, Physical/Mental Health, and Church Social Work. Special emphasis is given to low income populations and to issues related to spirituality and religion.

Student Organizations: Roberts Fellowship of MSW Students

Tips for Applicants: Areas examined include: emotional stability, self-confidence and assertiveness, ability to accept constructive criticism, intellectual ability, oral and written communication skills, interest in and motivation for the social work profession, ability to form and maintain positive relationships, ability to work with diverse groups, leadership qualities, values and ethics consistent with social work. Interest in issues related to spirituality and religion are important.

Common Applicant Mistakes: Applicants should make sure the autobiography addresses the items listed on the application instructions.

Saint Ambrose University School of Social Work, 518 West Locust Street, Davenport, IA 52803. Admissions Contact Person: Toni Wamsley. Phone: 319-333-6379. Fax: 319-333-6097. E-Mail: msw@saunix.sau.edu. Web Site Address: http://www.sau.edu/academic/MSW/MSWWEB.htm

Unique aspects of the program: Empowerment model, strengths perspective, social justice; small class sizes (less than 20) for more individualized instruction; faculty includes international empowerment scholars (Brenda DuBois, Michael O'Melia and Karla Miley); strong community and agency support; socially and politically active.

Student Organizations: Graduate Student Government Association; School of Social Work Student Association; Theta Sigma Chapter of Phi Alpha National Social Work Honor Society

Tips for Applicants: Applicants should demonstrate a strong commitment to social justice and a desire to work with the oppressed and populations-at-risk.

Common Applicant Mistakes: Poor writing skills; saying "I've always wanted to be a psychologist;" overwhelming religious motivations—"Want to do God's work," "called by God."

Saint Louis University School of Social Service, 3550 Lindell Boulevard, St. Louis, MO 63103. Admissions Contact Person: Gary Behrman. Phone: 314-977-2752. Fax: 314-977-2737. E-Mail: behrmang@slu.edu. Web Site Address: http://www.slu.edu/colleges/SOCSVC

Unique aspects of the program:

- Practice-focused curriculum in community, health, and family
- Center for Social Justice provides practice and research opportunities for students locally, nationally, and internationally
- Over 400 practicum sites and 800 practicum supervisors with a structured self-selection process
- Flexible scheduling with day, evening, and Saturday classes
- Small class size, friendly school, and available faculty for mentoring relationships
- Solid Jesuit education with required *Values and Ethics* course and social work values integrated throughout the curriculum
- Dual degree master's programs with Public Health and Pastoral Studies
- Integration of social work and spirituality available for students

Student Organizations: MSW Student Association; BSSW Student Association; Peace and Justice Commission; Black Social Work Student Association; Rainbow Alliance

Tips for Applicants: Well-developed writing skills and the ability to think and speak in a critical analytic manner are highly valued, as is a mature work experience that demonstrates responsibility and leadership.

Common Applicant Mistakes: Not following up with phone call or letter to determine status of application and not informing School about final decision on whether they will be attending.

Smith College School for Social Work, Admissions Office, Lilly Hall, Northampton, MA 01063. Admissions Contact Person: Ms. Sandra A. Austin, MSW, Director of Enrollment Management. Phone: 413-585-7960. Fax: 413-585-7994. E-Mail: sswadmis@smith.edu. Web Site Address: http://www.smith.edu/ssw

Unique aspects of the program: The MSW program is twenty-seven months in length and comprises three academic ten-week summer sessions and two intervening full-time eight-month field placements in 122 agencies affiliated with the School located in 22 states.

Student Organizations: The School has over two dozen groups that meet on campus during the summer academic terms.

Tips for Applicants: The School looks for students who have an interest in learning psychodynamic theories and desire to learn how to conduct clinical practice with individuals, families, or small groups. The School is interested in those applicants who have had an opportunity to explore their interest in the field. Applicants are considered when they have had about one year or more of paid or volunteer experience in human services.

Common Applicant Mistakes: Students that are unaware of the School's focus on clinical practice will request a concentration in a specific area (i.e., social policy).

Southern Illinois University at Carbondale School of Social Work, Quigley Hall, Carbondale, IL 62901-4329. Admissions Contact Person: Sandy Schenck. Phone: 618-453-2243. Fax: 618-453-1219. E-Mail: sandys@siu.edu. Web Site Address: http://www.siu.edu/~socwork/

Unique aspects of the program: Emphasis on community-based social services with concentrations in (1) Children, Youth, and Families and (2) Health/Mental Health. Also School Social Work. Concurrent degree program with law (JD). Strong emphasis on inter-professional education.

Student Organizations: Graduate Social Work Student Alliance

Tips for Applicants: Clear commitment to human services, particularly services to disadvantaged populations.

Common Applicant Mistakes: Poorly written personal statements; incomplete applications.

Southern Illinois University Edwardsville Department of Social Work, P. O. Box 1450, Edwardsville, IL 62026. Admissions Contact Person: Dr. Venessa Brown. Phone: 618-650-5758. Fax: 618-650-3509. Web Site Address: http://www.siue.edu/social/

Unique aspects of the program: Academic offerings include generalist practice in Children and Family Services and in Health, Mental Health, and Disabilities Services. Predominantly evening class schedule to accommodate nontraditional students.

Student Organizations: Graduate Students Social Work Association

Tips for Applicants: Commitment to practice with vulnerable at-risk populations.

Southwest Missouri State University School of Social Work, 901 South National Avenue, Springfield, MO 65804. Admissions Contact Person: Dr. John Gunther, Director. Phone: 417-836-5787. Fax: 417-836-7688. E-Mail: jog495f@mail.smsu.edu Web Site Address: http://www.smsu.edu/swk/

Unique aspects of the program: The only nationally accredited program in the United States offering a concentration in Family Health.

Student Organizations: MSW Club; Social Work Honor Society

Tips for Applicants: Rolling admissions policy; part-time and full-time programs.

Common Applicant Mistakes: Not looking at liberal arts prerequisites as requirements to admissions.

Spalding University, School of Professional Psychology and Social Work, 851 South Fourth Street, Louisville, KY 40203. Admissions Contact Person: Dr. Jillian Johnson, Chair of Department. Phone: 502-588-7183. Fax: 502-585-7159. E-Mail: gradadmissions@spalding.edu. Web Site Address: http://www.spalding.edu/graduate/socwrk/docmsw.htm.

Unique aspects of the program: The Spalding MSW is designed for adult learners balancing multiple responsibilities. Classes meet in a weekend intensive format, Friday at 6 p.m. until Sunday noon, approximately every other weekend, from late August through April. The program offers a single concentration in integrative social work practice to prepare advanced practitioners who sustain, throughout their careers and regardless of job title, agency setting, or preferred practice method, a consistent focus on both of social work's inherently interconnected purposes—human well-being and the alleviation of poverty and oppression. The concentration emphasizes critical reflective thinking and justice-promoting interventions in practice with diverse client systems. To insure that we "walk the talk," all faculty are active social work practitioners associated with local, regional, and national social justice movements.

Student Organizations: Graduate Social Work Student Association; National Association of Social Workers Student Chapter

Tips for Applicants: We smile when we meet an applicant who (1) is committed to working with society's most vulnerable members, (2) evidences the ability to participate in a rigorous graduate program, (3) demonstrates solid interpersonal skills, and (4) recognizes the need for planning and discipline to succeed in our intensive weekend format. Each year, we admit a cohort of only 50 students (25 regular program and 25 advanced), so we require a personal interview (which can be conducted by telephone) to build a genuinely diverse community of learners.

Common Applicant Mistakes: First, we want our applicants to be active participants in the admission process. Too often applicants are reluctant to raise questions or worries about the program or their admission status, thereby making it impossible for us to work together to solve problems. Speak up! Second, apply early! The weekend intensive format requires planning on both our parts. Applicants who have plenty of lead time appear to have an easier time making the transition to graduate school and developing strategies for balancing family, work, and academic responsibilities.

Springfield College School of Social Work, 263 Alden Street, Springfield, MA 01109. Admissions Contact: Office of Graduate Admissions. Phone: 413-748-3225. Fax: 413-748-3694. Web Site Address: http://www.spfldcol.edu

Unique aspects of the program: Advanced Generalist Concentration; Weekday MSW; Weekend MSW; Advanced Standing for qualified BSWs; MSW/JD combined degree program with Western New England College—open to full-time students.

Tips for Applicants: Springfield College looks for a personal statement describing (1) professional goals and reasons for pursuing an MSW degree in this program; and (2) the education, professional/work experience, and personal characteristics that make the applicant a good candidate for an advanced generalist MSW program.

Stephen F. Austin State University School of Social Work, P.O. Box 6104, SFA Station, Nacogdoches, TX 75962. Admissions Contact Person: Michael R. Daley, Director. Phone: 409-468-4020. Fax: 409-468-7201. E-Mail: mdaley@SFASU.edu. Web Site Address: http://www.sfasu.edu

Unique aspects of the program: The MSW concentration of Advanced Rural Generalist prepares students to work in a rural context.

Student Organizations: Association of Graduate Students in Social Work

Tips for Applicants: We look for students who are interested in working with rural people and/or rural communities. In addition, students should be interested in working with individuals, families, groups, organizations, and communities.

Common Applicant Mistakes: Failure to take the GRE (it is required by the Graduate School). Failure to take care with the personal statement of interest in social work.

Tulane University School of Social Work, 6823 St. Charles Avenue, New Orleans, LA 70118-5672. Admissions Contact Person: Lilia O. Valdez, Associate Dean. Phone: 504-865-5314. Fax: 504-862-8727. E-Mail: scholar@mailhost.tcs.tulane.edu. Web Site Address: http://www.tulane.edu/~tssw/

Unique aspects of the program: We offer a 16-month, four consecutive semester, MSW degree. Clinical focus with enhanced community development, advocacy and policy features. Year-long field placement in same agency allowing for in-depth experience. Center for Lifelong Learning; Visualization Center; Wisner Research Center; Tulane Center on Aging, Research, Education and Services; Disaster and Volunteerism Research Center; Gang Lloyd Institute: A Center for Research and Training in HIV/AIDS Social Work.

Student Organizations: Student Government Association; Diversity Coalition

Tips for Applicants: Strong analytical, critical, self-reflective written communication skills; commitment to social work ethics and values as demonstrated through paid/volunteer work experience.

Common Applicant Mistakes: Submitting poorly written, error filled personal statements; not addressing the questions in the autobiographical statement guidelines.

University of Alabama School of Social Work, Box 870314, Tuscaloosa, AL 35487-0314. Admissions Contact Person: Mary Alves Sella, Assistant for Student Services. Phone: 205-348-8557. Fax: 205-348-9419. E-Mail: msella@sw.ua.edu. Web Site Address: http://www.ua.edu/socwork/index.htm

Unique aspects of the program:

- Five concentration areas are offered: Health; Mental Health; Children, Youth, and Families; Aging; and Planning and Management

- Advanced Standing program for BSW graduates from CSWE-accredited programs
- Weekend College program—the first 21 semester hours can be completed on Saturdays
- The Washington Experience offers second-year students the opportunity to complete their field placements in the nation's capital. There are placements available in all concentration areas.
- Dual Degree program: MSW/MPH can be completed in two academic years, including two summers. It is offered in conjunction with the Department of Maternal and Child Health of the University of Alabama at Birmingham's School of Public Health.

Student Organizations: National Association of Black Social Workers (NABSW); Graduate Student Organization (open to all graduate students on campus). Each MSW class elects officers.

Tips for Applicants: The priority deadline for application for admission and scholarships is February 1 of the year when studies are to begin. The statement of purpose is carefully reviewed for both content and writing ability.

Common Applicant Mistakes: Incomplete application; late application; inadequate attention to the statement of purpose.

University of California at Berkeley School of Social Welfare, 120 Haviland Hall #7400, Berkeley, CA 94720-7400. Admissions Contact Person: Admissions Office. Phone: 510-642-9042. Fax: 510-643-6126. E-Mail: socwelf@uclink4.berkeley.edu. Web Site Address: http://hav54.socwel.berkeley.edu

Unique aspects of the program: Berkeley offers a demanding two-year full-time MSW program that educates social workers for a range of leadership and advanced practice roles in the profession. While students will be prepared to practice at specific intervention levels, and with specialized skills, all will be thoroughly grounded in a knowledge of social and psychological issues, social welfare policies, and social service organizations. Berkeley's educational emphasis is on preparing students for professional responsibility in the field of social welfare and the institutional systems that comprise it, particularly public social services and publicly supported voluntary social services. The modes of practice emphasized include those most relevant to the public service system.

Student Organizations: Social Welfare Graduate Assembly; American Indian Caucus; African American Caucus; Asian American Caucus; La Raza Caucus; Gay/Lesbian/Bisexual Caucus

Tips for Applicants:

- Contact the School and ask what their top candidate profile is and how competitive the specialization you are interested in is.
- Generally, substantial post-BA, social welfare related work experience will make your application more competitive.
- When you submit your application, verify that it is complete and all the pages that

require signatures have been signed. Keep in touch with the School until your application is complete.
- Take the GRE or TOEFL early and ensure that the School has received the scores.

Common Applicant Mistakes:

- Leaving out an application: You must submit BOTH the Graduate Application AND the Supplemental School of Social Welfare Application.
- Some applicants send in only BA transcripts. Make sure you send in ALL transcripts of college level coursework. It will delay processing if we do not have all transcripts.
- Incomplete applications are not reviewed, and we conduct a rolling admissions process. Making sure your application is complete and submitted early is to your advantage.

University of Central Florida, School of Social Work, P. O. Box 163358, Orlando, FL 32816-3358. Admissions Contact Person: Kenneth Kazmerski, Ph.D. Phone: 407-823-2114. Fax: 407-823-5697. Web Site Address: http://www.cohpa.ucf.edu/social/

Unique aspects of the program: The School of Social Work offers an advanced concentration in community-based clinical social work. It also offers a Graduate Certificate in Gerontology. Another certificate in Nonprofit Management is being developed. It offers part-time and full-time programs. International courses are Social Work in Mexico and Social Work in the Caribbean.

Student Organizations: MSW Club, CARE (student club promoting diversity)

Tips for Applicants: We are looking for students with a good academic background who share the value base and mission of social work. We also value work experience in social work and experiences that promote understanding of diversity.

Common Applicant Mistakes:

- Applying too late (after March 1)
- Making a poor selection of people for reference letters
- Believing that they can take a couple of classes to improve their undergraduate GPA (which is calculated on the basis of their BA degree and cannot be changed)

University of Chicago School of Social Service Administration, 969 East 60th Street, Chicago, IL 60637. Admissions Contact Person: Carlos A. Hernández, Director of Admissions. Phone: 773-702-1492. Fax: 773-834-1582. E-Mail: ssa_dos@uchicago.edu. Web Site Address: http://www.ssa.uchicago.edu/

Unique aspects of the program: Master of Arts in clinical and administrative social work; joint degrees in social work and divinity, business, and public policy; Ph.D. program; specialized programs in health administration and policy, family support, and school social work; part-time evening program; professional development program.

Student Organizations: Student Government Association; Extended Evening Program Student Government Association; African American Student Organization; Council of Jewish Social Work Students; Doctoral Student Association; Latino Student Association; Les-Bi-Gay Student Association; Pan Asian Student Association

Tips for Applicants: Call SSA Admissions Director for assistance. Applicants should be aware that SSA offers not only a strong program in administration of social work organizations but also a strong program in clinical social work (60% of SSA students are enrolled in the clinical program). Applicants should also be aware that 80% of students receive need and/or merit-based scholarships.

University of Georgia School of Social Work, Tucker Hall, Athens, GA 30602-7016. Admissions Contact Person: Ray H. MacNair, Director of MSW Admissions. Phone: 706-542=5421. Fax: 706-542-3282. E-Mail: mswadm@arches.uga.edu. Web Site Address: http://www.ssw.uga.edu

Unique aspects of the program: We have two concentrations: Family Centered Social Work Practice (Clinical) and Community Empowerment and Program Development.

Student Organizations: Student-Faculty Committee

Tips for Applicants: Our admissions criteria include emphasis on work history in the human services, experiences in cultural diversity, addressing social problems on multiple levels, and clarity and specificity of career objectives.

Common Applicant Mistakes: Getting materials in on the deadline date (March 1) and items come in late; taking the GRE late or only once.

University of Illinois at Urbana-Champaign School of Social Work, 1207 West Oregon Street, Urbana, IL 61801. Admissions Contact Person: Cindy Castañeda, Assistant Dean. Phone: 217-333-2261. Fax: 217-244-5240. E-Mail: social@uiuc.edu. Web Site Address: http://www.social.uiuc.edu

Unique aspects of the program: Specializations are available in direct practice as well as policy, planning, and administration in the following areas—Child Welfare, Mental Health, School Social Work, and Health Care. A unique dual degree program MSW/MS in Marriage and Family Studies is available. Students may elect field placements throughout Illinois.

Student Organizations: Graduate Social Work Association (GSWA)

Tips for Applicants: We recommend that students complete a statistics course with a "B" or better before starting the MSW program. All students must have completed 20 hours of social science courses as undergraduates and must have an undergraduate GPA of 3.0 or higher on 4.0 scale.

University of Iowa School of Social Work, 308 North Hall, Iowa City, IA 52242. Admissions Contact Person: Kate Kemp. Phone: 319-335-1259.

Fax: 319-335-1711. E-Mail: Kate-Kemp@uiowa.edu. Web Site Address: http://www.uiowa.edu/~socialwk

Unique aspects of the program: The Iowa School has a long tradition of innovation in social work education, research, and public service. Its National Resource Center on Family Based Services, Creative Writing Workshop, Child Welfare Traineeships, Mexican No-Poverty Seminar, Patch program (a federally funded community work demonstration project), and international journal of third world social development issues are among the unique features of the School. Integral to the School's history is the adherence to cross-disciplinary, cross-cultural, gender specific, and alternative life-style aspects of practice intervention and program development in social welfare. Poverty, ageism, racism, sexism, ethnic bias, and homophobia are addressed throughout the basic curriculum.

Student Organizations: The School of Social Work Graduate Student Association

Tips for Applicants: Professional experience is highly valued but not required.

Common Applicant Mistakes: Applicants do not always follow directions. GRE scores are required for application.

University of Kansas School of Social Welfare, Twente Hall, Lawrence, KS 66045-2510. Admissions Contact Person: Jan Lewis. Phone: 785-864-4720. Fax: 785-864-5277. E-Mail: janL@ukans.edu. Web Site Address: http://www.socwel.ukans.edu/

Unique aspects of the program: Education at the School of Social Welfare at the University of Kansas combines the profession's historic commitment to vulnerable people in our society with a value-based approach to social work practice.

University of Kentucky, College of Social Work, 615 Patterson Office Tower, Lexington, KY 40506-0027. Admissions Contact Person: Lynn Wallace. Phone: 606-257-6652. Fax: 606-323-1030. E-Mail: blwall1@pop.uky.edu. Web Site Address: http://www.uky.edu/SocialWork/welcome.html

Unique aspects of the program: The College of Social Work offers MSW courses for those who intend to go full time or part time. The part-time students attend evening courses. Full-time students may choose between day and evening sections. Applicants with high GPAs from accredited social work programs may qualify for the Advanced Standing Program, which requires 30 hours past the BSW. The Advanced Standing Program may be completed in two full-time semesters or three semesters and one summer as a part-time student.

Student Organizations: The Student Social Work Association (SSWA) participates in a number of activities from community service to fund raising, attending professional meetings and conventions, and even helping in the selection of new faculty.

Tips for Applicants: The College of Social Work is looking for solid students who are committed to helping others by using their heads, as well as their hearts.

Common Applicant Mistakes:

- Waiting too late to take the GRE
- Waiting until the last minute to get reference letters
- Not taking undergraduate studies seriously enough

University of Louisville Raymond A. Kent School of Social Work, Oppenheimer Hall, Louisville, KY 40292. Admissions Contact Person: Linda C. Chatmon, Director of Student Services. Phone: 502-852-6517 or 502-852-7162. Fax: 502-852-0422. Web Site Address: http://www.louisville.edu/kent/

Student Organizations: Kent School Student Association (KSSA)

Tips for Applicants: We look for students who can appreciate the opportunity to engage in a learning process that prepares them to become leaders in solving the problems of urban life by enhancing knowledge and skill development through blending theories of economics, politics, social policy, family systems, and psychology.

Common Applicant Mistakes: Failure to complete and/or sign the application; submission of non-official transcripts; submission of materials to other University offices instead of to the Kent School.

University of Maryland at Baltimore, School of Social Work, Louis L. Kaplan Hall, 525 W. Redwood Street, Baltimore, MD 21201. Admissions Contact Person: Marianne Wood, Assistant Dean. Phone: 410-706-3025. Fax: 410-706-7897. E-Mail: mwood@ssw.umaryland.edu. Web Site Address: http://ssw.umaryland.edu

Unique aspects of the program:

- Nationally ranked by *U.S. News & World Report*
- Faculty ranked #1 within the past 5 years as having published the most professional journal articles
- The first school-based social service agency (Social Work Community Outreach Service)
- Located in the urban area of Baltimore on an interprofessional campus that includes the schools of law, medicine, nursing, dentistry, and pharmacy

Student Organizations: Organization of African American Students in Social Work (OASIS); Student Council for Political and Economic Equity (SCOPE); Christian Social Work Fellowship (CSWF); Latin American Solidarity Organization (LASO); Student Government Association (SGA); Lesbian Gay Bi-Sexual Union (LGBU)

Tips for Applicants: We're looking for a diverse student body in terms of culture, race, gender, sexual orientation, and age.

Common Applicant Mistakes: Not reading application instructions thoroughly. Not developing the personal statement. Students with low GPAs don't submit test scores. Students send open transcripts, as opposed to in sealed envelopes, as requested.

University of Michigan School of Social Work, 1080 S. University Ave., Room 1748. Ann Arbor, MI 48109-1106. Admissions Contact Person: Tim Colenback, Assistant Director. Phone: 734-764-3309. Fax: 734-936-1961. E-Mail: ssw.msw.info@umich.edu. Web Site Address: http://www.ssw.umich.edu

Unique aspects of the program: Concentrations are available across a number of practice areas and methods. Practice areas include Adults and Elderly in Families and Society, Children and Youth in Families and Society, Community and Social Systems, Health, and Mental Health. Practice methods include Interpersonal Practice, Community Organization, Management of Human Services, and Social Policy and Evaluation. Specialization and Certificate options include Specialist in Aging Certificate, Certificate in Jewish Communal Service and Judaic Studies, Social Work in the Public Schools, and Social Work in the Workplace. Doctoral programs in social work and social science are also offered.

Curriculum schedules include Advanced Standing (12-month schedule), 16-month schedule, 20-month schedule, Fifth Term Option, and the Extended Degree Program.

Dual degree options include Social Work and Business Administration, Social Work and Law, Social Work and Public Health, Social Work and Public Policy, and Social Work and Urban Planning.

Student Organizations: Social Work Student Union; Association of Black Social Work Students (ABSWS); Rainbow Network; Coalition of Asian Social Work Students; Social Work International Students in Action; Civitas Action Coalition; Michigan Gerontological Society; Adventure Based Counseling; Bertha Reynolds Society; School Social Work Club; Doctoral Student Organization; Student Organization of Latina/o Social Workers (SOLASW)

Tips for Applicants: Admissions decisions are based primarily on an evaluation of previous undergraduate and graduate work, recommendations, experience in the human services (paid, volunteer, research, and internship) and the applicant's written supplementary statement.

Common Applicant Mistakes: Waiting until the priority deadline to apply; delaying completion of financial aid application; failing to address all of the questions in the supplementary statement.

University of Minnesota—Duluth, Department of Social Work, 220 Bohannon Hall, Duluth, MN 55812. Admissions Contact Person: Dr. Joyce Kramer. Phone: 218-726-7245 or 888-534-9734. Fax: 218-726-7185. E-Mail: sw@d.umn.edu. Web Site Address: http://www.d.umn.edu/~sw/

Unique aspects of the program: UMD's graduate program in social work is one of the few programs in the country offering an Advanced Generalist Concentration. This provides students with an integrated professional knowledge base, which prepares them to practice at the direct service, administrative, and community levels. The program also provides opportunities to focus on Child Welfare Practice and offers a Child Welfare Scholar's Program. The curriculum also has a special focus on American Indian Social Services.

Student Organizations: MSW Student Association

Tips for Applicants: Students should have a commitment to working with diverse populations and to developing as culturally competent professionals. Students interested and/or experienced in child welfare practice and working with American Indian populations are encouraged to apply.

Common Applicant Mistakes: Incomplete application materials; failure to demonstrate their commitment to working with diverse populations.

University of Missouri–Columbia, School of Social Work, 723 Clark Hall—UMC, Columbia, MO 65211. Admissions Contact Person: Tammy Freelin, Student Services Coordinator. Phone: 573-882-6208. Fax: 573-882-8926. E-Mail: FreelinT@missouri.edu. Web Site Address: http://www.missouri.edu/~sswmain/

Unique aspects of the program: Concentrations are available in planning and administration, mental health services, family and children services, and physical health services. Rural social work emphasis is available. The School is a Charter Member of the Council on Social Work Education. Course scheduling is designed to accommodate part-time and commuter students, and there is a 37-hour Advanced Standing program.

Student Organizations: Council of Student Social Workers (CSSW), Phi Alpha-Chi Delta Chapter

Tips for Applicants: Make sure your personal statement is thoughtful and well-written. It is our best opportunity to learn about who you are and why you want an MSW.

Common Applicant Mistakes: Not getting all items in by the deadline, including GRE scores, transcripts, and references.

University of New England School of Social Work, 11 Hills Beach Road, Biddeford, ME 04005. Admissions Contact Person: Joanne Thompson. Phone: 207-283-0171. Fax: 207-284-7633. E-Mail: jthompson@mailbox.une.edu. Web Site Address: http://www.une.edu/chp/ssw/sswhome.htm

Unique aspects of the program: Students have an opportunity to specialize in clinical or integrated practice. Both concentrations emphasize a strengths perspective and students acquiring skills in implementing change across all systems levels. The School is also developing opportunities to explore social work through the arts and international exchanges.

Student Organizations: School Student Organization

Tips for Applicants: Applications are reviewed for life experiences, applicant's understanding and support of the School's Mission Statement, a commitment to social justice and the alleviation of all forms of oppression. The applicant's personal statement is very important.

Common Applicant Mistakes: Insufficient attention to the School's Mission Statement; inadequate completion of personal statement.

University of New Hampshire Department of Social Work, Murkland Hall 25, 15 Library Way, Durham, NH 03824. Admissions Contact Person: Elizabeth Forshay, Admissions Coordinator. Phone: 603-862-0076. Fax: 603-862-4374. E-Mail: eforshay@hopper.unh.edu. Web Site Address: http://www.unh.edu/social-work/index.html

Unique aspects of the program: We are a new and growing program recently accredited by CSWE. Faculty research and interests range from child welfare to gerontology to evaluation of welfare reform. We are the first MSW program in New Hampshire.

Student Organizations: Graduate Organization of Social Work Students

Tips for Applicants: The admissions committee looks at transcripts, references, work experience, and personal statements. Personal statements are very important—they are the one chance for the admissions committee to get to know the applicant.

Common Applicant Mistakes: The most common mistake is not including all relevant social services and work experience. We would like to know about volunteer and work experience—it is often helpful to include a résumé.

University of North Carolina at Chapel Hill School of Social Work, Tate-Turner-Kuralt Building, 301 Pittsboro Street, CB 3550, Chapel Hill, NC 27599-3550. Admissions Contact Person: Linda T. Wilson, Administrative Assistant for Student Services. Phone: 919-962-6442. Fax: 919-843-8562. E-Mail: ltw2517@email.unc.edu. Web Site Address: http://ssw.unc.edu

Unique aspects of the program: The UNC-CH School of Social Work, established in 1920, offers MSW and Ph.D. degrees. Students in the fully-accredited master's program prepare for agency-based practice in public and nonprofit settings, with special emphasis on work in the public sector. Students in the Ph.D. program prepare for research and teaching roles. The specific emphasis of the School's educational program is to prepare students for roles in strengthening families across fields of practice. The School's educational mission recognizes the uniqueness of the region served, showing concern for oppressed groups with special emphasis on women and on African Americans, on the causes and effects of poverty, and on provision of services in rural areas. An online application is located at the School's Web site.

Student Organizations: The primary student organization is SoWoSO. Students have representation on all major school committees and they organize special interest groups such as Social Justice Caucus, Black Student Caucus, Women's Caucus, and others. Students also have a major role in the Hunger Banquet, the Art Show (displaying work of clients), and the Student Health Action Committee, which runs a free clinic.

Tips for Applicants: Experience in human services is important, because it shows applicants have organized their lives so that their volunteer and work experience reflects interest in human behavior, social problems, and community change strategies.

Applicants have real experience to write about in their narrative, and they have people who can write references that reflect their skills and abilities as potential social workers.

Common Applicant Mistakes: Overlooking how competitive the program is; not taking personal responsibility to make sure all the pieces of the application are completed, especially the references; waiting until the last minute, which does not allow time to take the GRE or write a proper narrative statement.

University of Oklahoma School of Social Work, 1005 Jenkins Avenue, Norman, OK 73019. Admissions Contact Person: Dr. Jim Rosenthal, Professor and Graduate Coordinator. Phone: 405-325-2821. Fax: 405-325-7072. E-Mail: jimar@ou.edu. Web Site Address: http://www.ou.edu/socialwork

Unique aspects of the program: Opportunities for stipends in child welfare, tuition waiver possibilities, full-time and part-time program options, advanced standing option for BSW graduates.

Student Organizations: Graduate Social Work Student Association, American Indian Social Work Student Association

Tips for Applicants: The School seeks applicants with a strong commitment to social work ethics and values, including social justice, and a motivation to work with oppressed and disadvantaged groups and persons. It seeks to build a learning community comprised of persons from diverse backgrounds.

Common Applicant Mistakes: Delaying taking of the GRE, not paying sufficient attention to prerequisite course requirements, missing priority application deadlines (February 1 for general University materials and March 1 for social work-specific materials).

University of Pittsburgh School of Social Work, 2103 Cathedral of Learning, 5th and Bigelow, Pittsburgh, PA 15260. Admissions Contact Person: Grady Henry Roberts, Jr., Ph.D., Assistant Dean. Phone: 412-624-6302. Fax: 412-624-6323. Web site address: http://www.pitt.edu/~pittsw/

Unique aspects of the program: The Center for Mental Health Services Research (CMHSR) at the University is one of seven national social work research development centers funded by the National Institute of Mental Health. An interdisciplinary initiative, the CMHSR capitalizes on the School of Social Work's extensive knowledge of the community and the Department of Psychiatry's clinical research expertise. Emphasis is on the identification and study of variables that facilitate or hinder the effective use of mental health treatment services, including access to care and adherence to treatment.

Student Organizations: Student Executive Council (SEC), Black Action Society (BAS), Community Organization Group (COG), Bachelor of Arts in Social Work Club (BASW)

Tips for Applicants: We look for students who are mature, have earned an excellent academic record, have good interpersonal skills, a good work ethic, commitment to the social work profession, and a positive attitude.

Common Applicant Mistakes: A common mistake is waiting until the last day of the application period before submitting application materials.

University of South Carolina College of Social Work, Columbia, SC 29208. Admissions Contact Person: Dr. John T. Gandy, Associate Dean. Phone: 803-777-3599. Fax: 803-777-3498. Web Site Address: http://www.sc.edu/cosw/

Unique aspects of the program: Our master's program includes both full- and part-time options, distance education courses through interactive television, and the specialization options of individuals/families/groups or organizations/communities.

Student Organizations: Social Work Student Association, Black Social Work Student Association

Tips for Applicants: Admission is competitive. Students are advised to make their application as strong as possible.

Common Applicant Mistakes: Some applicants do not respond to all items and leave parts of the application blank. Applicants should respond thoroughly to all items.

The University of Southern Mississippi School of Social Work, Box 5114, Hattiesburg, MS 39406. Admissions Contact Person: Michael Forster. Phone: 601-266-4163. Fax: 601-266-4165. E-Mail: michael.forster@usm.edu. Web Site Address: http://www-dept.usm.edu/~socwork/

Unique aspects of the program: We are among a relatively small number of programs that offer the "advanced generalist" concentration. In contrast to concentrations in, for example, child welfare, or administration, the advanced generalist curriculum prepares MSWs to address complex, multi-dimensional problems in a full range of contexts spanning the five systems of individual, family, group, organization, and community. We believe that the advanced generalist is an especially appropriate preparation for social workers who expect to practice in settings with limited professional resources.

Student Organizations: Student Association of Social Workers, Phi Alpha Honor Society

Tips for Applicants: Applicants should develop strong personal statements that reflect the applicant's motivation to pursue a professional social work career, a clear appreciation of the value base of the profession, and, ideally, life experiences that illustrate the applicant's commitment to addressing injustice, oppression, and other social problems.

Common Applicant Mistakes: Our process calls for the applicant to submit most application materials, including reference letters, in one package to the School. A common mistake of applicants is to submit materials piecemeal. Another common mistake is to submit weak reference letters from family friends or others who cannot effectively speak to either the academic or professional promise of the applicant.

University of Tennessee College of Social Work, 112 Henson Hall, Admissions Office, Knoxville, TN 37996-3333. Admissions Contact Person: Sylvia A. Nash, Administrative Services Assistant. Phone: 423-974-6697. Fax: 423-974-4803. E-Mail: snash@utk.edu. Web Site Address: http://www.csw.utk.edu

Unique aspects of the program: Full MSSW program available on 3 campuses: Knoxville, Nashville, and Memphis. Full-time, Extended Study, and Advanced Standing programs available. Two concentrations are Clinical Social Work and Management and Community Practice. Field placements are available in the regions surrounding each campus. The College of Social Work has the Children's Mental Health Research Center.

Student Organizations: MSSW Student Social Work Organization on each campus

Tips for Applicants: Preference is given to applicants with a GPA of 3.0 or above in their undergraduate work, appropriate preparation in the social sciences, and work or volunteer experience directly related to the field of social work.

Common Applicant Mistakes: Sending materials to the wrong address; assuming that requested transcripts and reference evaluation forms have actually been received by the College. You may call us to check what has been received.

University of Texas at Arlington School of Social Work, Box 19129, Arlington, TX 76019-0129. Admissions Contact Person: Norma B. Cole, Director of Admissions. Phone: 817-272-3552. Fax: 817-272-5229. E-Mail: benavi@uta.edu. Web Site Address: http://www2.uta.edu/ssw/

Unique aspects of the program: The School of Social Work provides tremendous options of advanced course electives. Students have the option to select advanced courses. We offer a strong cognitive-behavioral program. We provide over 300 field placement opportunities in the Dallas/Fort Worth area. We also offer a unique legislative intern program. We provide biofeedback courses leading to certification. We also provide extensive audio visual instruction. Courses are offered across 12 hours during day and evening hours.

Student Organizations: Social Work Constituency Club, National Association of Social Workers Student Chapter

Tips for Applicants: We are looking for mature students who are focused on social work careers. We seek applicants who are dedicated to the goals and ethics of social work, independent, self-motivated, self-directed, and who work well with mentors.

Common Applicant Mistakes: Applicants sometimes do not familiarize themselves thoroughly with requirements for admission. Some take too long to submit transcripts and do not follow up to make sure materials have been sent (particularly letters of recommendation).

University of Utah, Graduate School of Social Work, 395 S. 1500 East, Room 101, Salt Lake City, UT 84112-0260. Admissions Contact Person: Professor Larry Smith. Phone: 801-581-5103. Fax: 801-585-3219. E-Mail: lsmith@socwk.utah.edu. Web Site Address: http://www.socwk.utah.edu/

Unique aspects of the program: Concentration in family and community practice

Student Organizations: Associated Students of the Graduate School of Social Work

Tips for Applicants: The School looks for maturity, commitment, and experience in the human services.

Common Applicant Mistakes: Incomplete application; missing the deadline.

University of Vermont Department of Social Work, 228 Waterman Building, Burlington, VT 05405. Admissions Contact Person: Kendra Pineda-Massari, MSW, Admissions Coordinator. Phone: 802-656-8800 or 802-656-4322. Fax: 802-656-8565. E-Mail: kpinedam@zoo.uvm.edu. Web Site Address: http://www.uvm.edu/~socwork/index.html

Unique aspects of the program: UVM's MSW program's mission is based upon a set of core, interrelated beliefs that provide an orientation to the way in which social work is understood and practiced. We identify these beliefs as the strengths perspective, critical constructionism, social justice, and human rights. Students will find these perspectives integrated throughout the curriculum. Also, the program provides opportunities for field work/internships in rural as well as more urban settings.

Student Organizations: Student Social Work Organization, ALANA

Tips for Applicants: It is recommended that applicants clearly demonstrate their understanding of social work as a profession and their particular interest in applying to UVM's MSW program.

Common Applicant Mistakes: Having all three references from academic sources or all three from professional sources (there should be a balance between the two sources); not clearly articulating their commitment to social work as a profession and/or their interest in UVM's program in particular.

Virginia Commonwealth University School of Social Work, 1001 W. Franklin St., P.O. Box 842027, Richmond, VA 23284-2027. Admissions Contact Person: Dr. Ann Nichols-Casebolt, Associate Dean. Phone: 804-828-0703. Fax: 804-828-0716. E-Mail: ssw.info@vcu.edu. Web Site Address: http://www.vcu.edu/slwweb/index.htm

Unique aspects of the program: Virginia Commonwealth University is a major urban institution located in Richmond, VA. The School of Social Work offers concentrations in clinical social work practice and planning and administrative practice. Other special offerings are a dual degree program in law and social work and certificate programs in gerontology, early childhood intervention, and school social work. An advanced standing program is offered to qualified applicants.

Student Organizations: MSW Student Association, Part Time Student Association, Black Student Association, Sexual Minority Student Association, Students with Disabilities Association

Tips for Applicants: Applicants should communicate well through their personal statement a commitment to the social work profession that is consistent with the mission of the School.

Common Applicant Mistakes: Incomplete application packets (missing materials); failure to submit materials by the deadline; not including copies of all transcripts from all undergraduate universities/colleges attended.

Washington University, George Warren Brown School of Social Work, One Brookings Drive, Campus Box 1196, St. Louis, MO 63130. Admissions Contact Person: Brian W. Legate. Phone: 314-935-6676. Fax: 314-935-4859. E-Mail: mswadmis@gwbssw.wustl.edu. Web Site Address: http://gwbweb.wustl.edu

Unique aspects of the program: Ranked by *U.S. News & World Report* as tied for the top school of social work in the nation; outstanding faculty; talented and idealistic students from 44 states and 22 foreign countries; extensive financial aid, including over 125 merit-based scholarships; a challenging curriculum combining theory, policy, practice methods, evaluation techniques, and skills training; six concentrations (children, youth, and families; gerontology; health; mental health; social and economic development; and individually designed concentration); three specializations (family therapy, management, and research); dual degrees with law, business, architecture, and Jewish communal studies; possibilities of international field placements; specialized career planning and placement services; world-class facilities, including state-of-the-art technology and one of the best social work libraries in the country; excellent research opportunities through our three research centers: Center for Mental Health Services Research, Center for Social Development, and the Kathryn M. Buder Center for American Indian Studies.

Student Organizations: Student Coordinating Committee (Student Government), All Nations Christian Fellowship (ANCF), Asian and Pacific Islanders Issues Association (APIA), ACCESS Washington University, Buder Center for American Indian Studies, FOCUSED on Social Justice, Gerontology Students Association, GLOBE, International Scope, JD/MSW Student Group, Men's Wellness Group, NASW Student Association, Non-Traditional Students, Nosotros (Hispanic Issue and Outreach Group), Outlook, Radical Action (for) Women (RAW), School Social Workers, Society of Black Student Social Workers (SBSSW), Voices for Children, Women's Issues Network (WIN)

Tips for Applicants: Unique factors looked for include (1) demonstrated potential for future leadership in the social work profession and (2) outstanding academic background.

Common Applicant Mistakes: Not submitting all required information; misspelled words, typos, or incorrect punctuation in essays; late applications; lack of academic or professional references.

Wayne State University School of Social Work, 4756 Cass Avenue, Detroit, MI 48202. Admissions Contact Person: Ms. Anwar Najor-Durack. Phone: 313-577-4409. Fax: 313-577-4266. E-Mail: ac1724@wayne.edu. Web Site Address: http://www.socialwork.wayne.edu

Unique aspects of the program: The WSU School of Social Work is located in the heart of the cultural center of the City of Detroit. The environment is multicultural and urban. It is uniquely set in an environment that supports addressing urban issues of economic and social justice. There are large populations of African-Americans, Latinos, Arabs, and Chaldeans. There are identifiable communities of Polish, Irish, Greek, and Italian peoples. Detroit is a border town between the USA and Canada, which brings the global perspective to the front doors of the School. The environment is exciting and intellectually stimulating. Wayne's faculty, staff, and students are very diverse in their ethnic origins and areas of interest. It is a supportive environment for collaborative learning and sharing. Wayne faculty are known for their expertise in teaching and their accessibility to students and alumni.

Student Organizations: The student organizations at Wayne reflect the School's diversity: Student Organization, National Association of Black Social Workers, Student Organization of Latino/a Social Workers, Christian Fellowship Group, Jewish Interest Group, Bi-sexual/Gay/Lesbian and Allies in Social Work, Arab/Chaldean Interest Group, and Single Parents Support Group.

Tips for Applicants: Documented support of applicant's commitment to social and economic justice, interest in urban social work practice, and paid or volunteer experience in the human services. Evidence of the ability to communicate verbally and in writing is important.

Common Applicant Mistakes: Some applicants fail to attend an MSW information meeting and do not read the instructions in the application packet, thus producing an application file that is not as competitive as it could be. Other mistakes include not taking the time to compose a strong application or to carefully edit their Personal Interest Statement, and being careless with the completion of their comprehensive résumé. Waiting until the last day to apply is another mistake.

Widener University Center for Social Work Education, One University Place, Chester, PA 19013. Admissions Contact Person: Paula Silver, Ph.D., Associate Dean and Director. Phone: 610-499-1153. Fax: 610-499-4617. E-Mail: paula.t.silver@widener.edu. Web Site Address: http://muse.widener.edu/SocialWork/

Unique aspects of the program: Widener University offers a single concentration in agency-based clinical social work designed to prepare students for advanced clinical practice with individuals, families, and small groups. The program has two admissions options—Regular (62 credits) and Advanced Standing (39 credits), which is for students holding a BSW from an accredited BSW program. Both regular and advanced standing students may opt for full-time or part-time study.

Student Organizations: MSW Student Organization; Association of Black Social Workers, Student Chapter; SAGA (Straight and Gay Alliance)

Tips for Applicants: Well-written and self-reflective personal statement essay; volunteer or work experience in human services; clear understanding of reasons for selecting graduate social work training.

Common Applicant Mistakes: Applying too late; poorly written application materials.

Yeshiva University Wurzweiler School of Social Work, 2495 Amsterdam Avenue, New York, NY 10033. Admissions Contact Person: Michele Sarracco. Phone: 212-960-0820. Fax: 212-960-0822. E-Mail: wsswadmissions@ymail.yu.edu. Web Site Address: http://www.yu.edu/wurzweiler

Unique aspects of the program: Program for employed social service personnel with evening and Sunday classes; Summer Block program; certificate in Jewish Communal Service.

Student Organizations: Student Government, Bridging the Gap

Appendix D

State Social Work Boards

The material in this Appendix is reprinted with permission of the American Association of State Social Work Boards (AASSWB) and is current as of October 1999. For more information, contact AASSWB, 400 South Ridge Parkway, Suite B, Culpeper, Virginia 22701. Telephone (800) 225-6880 or (540) 829-6880, Fax (540) 829-0142. E-Mail: info@aasswb.org. Web: http://www.aasswb.org.

ALABAMA

State Board of Social Work Examiners
Folsom Administrative Building
64 North Union Street, Suite 129
Montgomery, AL 36130
334-242-5860

Title	**Education**	**Experience**	**AASSWB Exam**
Private Independent Practice (PIP)	DSW / MSW	2 yrs POST	N/R (Board Review)
Licensed Certified Social Worker (LCSW)	DSW / MSW	2 yrs POST	Clinical/Advanced
Licensed Graduate Social Worker (LGSW)	MSW	None	Intermediate
Licensed Bachelor Social Worker (LBSW)	BSW	None	Basic

ALASKA

Board of Clinical Social Work Examiners
Division of Occupational Licensing
P. O. Box 110806
Juneau, AK 99811-0806
907-465-2551

Title	Education	Experience	AASSWB Exam
Licensed Clinical Social Worker (LCSW)	DSW/MSW	2 yrs POST	Clinical

ARIZONA

Board of Behavioral Health Examiners
1400 West Washington, #350
Phoenix, AZ 85007
602-542-1882
http://aspin.asu.edu/~azbbhe

Title	Education	Experience	AASSWB Exam
Certified Independent Social Worker (CISW)	DSW/MSW	2 yrs POST	Clin/Adv
Certified Master Social Worker (CMSW)	DSW/MSW	None	Intermediate
Certified Baccalaureate Social Worker (BSW)	BSW	None	Basic

ARKANSAS

Social Work Licensing Board
2020 West Third Street, Suite 503
P. O. Box 250381
Little Rock, AR 72225
501-372-5071

Title	Education	Experience	AASSWB Exam
Licensed Certified Social Worker (LCSW)	MSW	2 yrs POST	Clin/Adv
Licensed Master Social Worker (LMSW)	MSW	None	Intermediate
Licensed Social Worker (LSW)	BSW	None	Basic

CALIFORNIA

Board of Behavioral Science Examiners
400 R Street, Suite 3150
Sacramento, CA 95814-6240
916-445-4933
http://www.bbs.ca.gov

Title	Education	Experience	AASSWB Exam
Licensed Clinical Social Worker (LCSW)	MSW	2 yrs POST	State specific exam*

Associate Clinical Social Worker (ASW)	MSW	None	N/R

*oral exam also required. AASSWB exam not accepted in California.

COLORADO

Board of Social Work Examiners
1560 Broadway, Suite 1340
Denver, CO 80202
303-894-7766

Title	Education	Experience	AASSWB Exam
Licensed Clinical Social Worker (LCSW)	DSW or MSW	1 yr POST 2 yrs POST	Clinical/Advanced Clinical/Advanced
Licensed Independent Social Worker (LISW)	DSW or MSW	1 yr POST 2 yrs POST	Clinical/Advanced Clinical/Advanced
Licensed Social Worker (LSW)	MSW	None	Intermediate
Registered Social Worker (RSW)	BSW	None	Basic

CONNECTICUT

Department of Public Health
Social Work Regulation
410 Capitol Avenue, MS #12APP.
Hartford, CT 06314-0308
860-509-7567

Title	Education	Experience	AASSWB Exam
Licensed Clinical Social Worker (LCSW)	DSW /MSW	3000 hrs POST	Clinical

DELAWARE

Board of Clinical Social Work Examiners
Cannon Bldg. Suite 203
861 Silverlake Boulevard
Dover, DE 19904-2467
302-739-4522 ext 220

Title	Education	Experience	AASSWB Exam
Licensed Clinical Social Worker (LCSW)	DSW /MSW	2 yrs POST	Clinical

DISTRICT OF COLUMBIA

Board of Social Work
D.C. Department of Health
Office of Professional Licensing
825 N. Capitol Street, NE, Room 2204
Washington, DC 20001
202-442-9200
http://www.dcra.org

Title	Education	Experience	AASSWB Exam
Licensed Independent Clinical Social Worker (LICSW)	MSW	3000 hrs POST	Clinical
Licensed Independent Social Worker (LCSW)	MSW	3000 hrs POST	Advanced
Licensed Graduate Social Worker (LGSW)	MSW	None	Intermediate
Licensed Social Work Associate (LSWA)	BSW	None	Basic

FLORIDA

Board of Clinical Social Work, Marriage and Family Therapy, and Mental Health Counseling
2020 Capital Circle, SE, BIN #C08
Tallahassee, FL 32399-3258
850-488-0595

Title	Education	Experience	AASSWB Exam
Licensed Clinical Social Worker (LCSW)	DSW/MSW	2 yrs POST	Clinical
Certified Master Social Worker (CMSW)	MSW	2 yrs POST	Intermediate

GEORGIA

Composite Board of Professional Counselors, Social Workers, and Marriage & Family Therapists
237 Coliseum Drive
Macon, GA 31217-3858
912-207-1670
http://www.sos.state.ga.us/ebd-counselors

Title	Education	Experience	AASSWB Exam
Licensed Clinical Social Worker (LCSW)	MSW	3 yrs POST	Clinical/Advanced
Licensed Master Social Worker (LMSW)	MSW	None	Intermediate

HAWAII

Department of Commercial Consumer Affairs
P.O. Box 3469
Honolulu, HI 96813
808-586-3000

Title	Education	Experience	AASSWB Exam
Licensed Social Worker (LSW)	DSW/MSW	None	Intermediate

IDAHO

State Board of Social Work Examiners
Bureau of Occupational Licensing
Owyhee Plaza-1109 Main Street, Suite 220
Boise, ID 83702
208-334-3233

Title	Education	Experience	AASSWB Exam
Independent Practice (CSW)	DSW/MSW	2 yrs POST	Intermediate
Certified Social Worker (CSW)	DSW/MSW	None	Intermediate
Social Worker (SW)	BSW	None	Basic

ILLINOIS

Social Work Examining and Disciplinary Board
Department of Professional Regulation
320 West Washington Street, 3rd Floor
Springfield, IL 62786
217-785-0800

Title	Education	Experience	AASSWB Exam
Licensed Clinical	DSW	2000 hrs POST	Clinical
Social Worker (LCSW)	or MSW	3000 hrs POST	Clinical
Licensed Social	MSW	None	Intermediate
Worker (LSW)	or BSW	3 yrs POST	Intermediate

INDIANA

Social Work Certification and Marriage & Family Therapists Credentialing Board
Health Professions Bureau
Indiana Government Center
402 West Washington Street, Room 041
Indianapolis, IN 46204
317-233-4422

Title	Education	Experience	AASSWB Exam
Licensed Clinical Social Worker (LCSW)	MSW	2000 hrs POST	Clinical
Licensed Social Worker (LSW)	MSW	None	Intermediate
	or BSW	2 yrs POST	Intermediate

IOWA

Board of Social Work Examiners
Bureau of Professional Licensure
Lucas State Office Building
321 E. 12th Street
Des Moines, IA 50319-0075
515-281-4422

Title	Education	Experience	AASSWB Exam
Licensed Independent Social Worker (LISW)	DSW/MSW	2 yrs POST	Clinical
Licensed Master Social Worker (LMSW)	DSW/MSW	None	Intermediate
Licensed Bachelor Social Worker (LBSW)	BSW	None	Basic

KANSAS

Behavioral Sciences Regulatory Board
712 S. Kansas Avenue
Topeka, KS 66603-3817
785-296-3240

Title	Education	Experience	AASSWB Exam
Specialist Clinical Social Worker (LSCSW)	DSW/MSW	2 yrs POST	Clinical
Master Social Worker (MSW)	MSW	None	Intermediate
Baccalaureate Social Worker (BSW)	BSW	None	Basic

KENTUCKY

Board of Examiners of Social Work
Berry Hill Annex
Louisville Road, Box 456
Frankfort, KY 40602
502-564-3296

Title	Education	Experience	AASSWB Exam
Licensed Independent Practice (LCSW)	DSW/MSW	2 yrs POST	Clinical
Certified Social Worker (CSW)	MSW	None	Intermediate
Licensed Social Worker (LSW)	BSW	None	Basic
	or BA	2 yrs	Basic

LOUISIANA

State Board of BCSW Examiners
11930 Perkins Road, Suite B
Baton Rouge, LA 70810
225-763-5470
http://www.labswe.org

Title	Education	Experience	AASSWB Exam
Board Certified Social Worker (BCSW)	MSW	2 yrs POST	Clinical/Advanced

MAINE

State Board of Social Work Licensure
35 State House Station
Augusta, ME 04333
207-624-8603

Title	Education	Experience	AASSWB Exam
Licensed Clinical Social Worker (LCSW)	DSW/MSW	2 yrs POST	Clinical
Licensed Master Social Worker (LMSW)	DSW/MSW	None	Intermediate
Licensed Social Worker (LSW)	BSW	None	Basic
	or BA/BS	3200 hrs	Basic

MARYLAND

State Board of Social Work Examiners
Department of Health and Mental Hygiene
4201 Patterson Avenue
Baltimore, MD 21215-2299
410-764-4788
http://www.dhmh.state.md.us/bswe/

Title	Education	Experience	AASSWB Exam
Licensed Certified Social Worker—Clinical (LCSW)	DSW/MSW	2 yrs POST	Clinical
Licensed Certified	DSW/MSW	2 yrs POST	Advanced

Social Worker (LCSW)			
Licensed Graduate Social Worker (LGSW)	DSW/MSW	None	Intermediate
Licensed Social Work Associate (LSW)	BSW	None	Basic

MASSACHUSETTS **Commonwealth of Massachusetts**
Division of Registration
239 Causeway Street
Boston, MA 02114
617-727-3073
http://www.state.ma.us/reg/boards/

Title	**Education**	**Experience**	**AASSWB Exam**
Licensed Independent Clinical Social Worker (LICSW)	DSW/MSW	3 yrs	Clinical
Licensed Certified	DSW	None	Intermediate
Social Worker (LCSW)	or MSW	3 yrs POST	Intermediate
Licensed Social Worker (LSW)	BSW	None	Basic
	or BA	2 yrs	Basic
	or 1 yr college	5 yrs	Basic
	or HS	8 yrs	Basic
Licensed Certified Social Worker (LSWA)	AA/BA	None	Associate

MICHIGAN **Board of Examiners of Social Work**
611 W. Ottowa Street
P. O. Box 30246
Lansing, MI 48909
517-241-9245

Title	**Education**	**Experience**	**AASSWB Exam**
Certified Social Worker (CSW)	MSW	2 yrs POST	Not Required
Social Worker (SW)	MSW	2 yrs POST	Not Required
	or BA	2 yrs POST	Not Required
Social Work	2 yrs college	1 yr POST	Not Required
Technician (SWT)	or 1 yr exp	1 yr	Not Required

MINNESOTA **Board of Social Work Examiners**
2829 University Avenue, SE, Suite 340
Minneapolis, MN 55414-3239
612-617-2100

Title	Education	Experience	AASSWB Exam
Licensed Independent Clinical Social Worker (LICSW)	DSW/MSW	2 yrs POST	Clinical
Licensed Independent Social Worker (LISW)	DSW/MSW	2 yrs POST	Advanced
Licensed Graduate Social Worker (LGSW)	MSW	None	Intermediate
Licensed Social Worker (LSW)	BSW	None	Basic

MISSISSIPPI

Board of Examiners for Social Workers
And Marriage & Family Therapists
P.O. Box 4508
Jackson, MS 39215-4508
601-987-6806

Title	Education	Experience	AASSWB Exam
Licensed Certified Social Worker (LCSW)	DSW/MSW	2 yrs POST	Clinical/Advanced
Licensed Master Social Worker (LMSW)	DSW/MSW	None	Intermediate
Licensed Social Worker (LSW)	BSW	None	Basic

MISSOURI

State Committee for Licensed Social Workers
Division of Professional Registration
3605 Missouri Blvd.
P.O. Box 1335
Jefferson City, MO 65102
573-751-0885
http://www.ecodev.state.mo.us/pr/social

Title	Education	Experience	AASSWB Exam
Licensed Clinical Social Worker (LCSW)	DSW/MSW	2 yrs POST	Clinical/Advanced

MONTANA

Board of Social Work Examiners
Arcade Building
111 North Jackson
PO Box 200513
Helena, MT 59620-0407
406-444-4285

http://www.com.state.mt.us/License/POL/index.htm

Title	Education	Experience	AASSWB Exam
Licensed Social Worker (LSW)	DSW/MSW	2 yrs POST	Clinical/Advanced

NEBRASKA

Bureau of Examining Boards
301 Centennial Mall South
P. O. Box 94986
Lincoln, NE 68509-4986
402-471-2117

Title	Education	Experience	AASSWB Exam
Certified Mental Health Practitioner (CMHP)	MA (Mental Health)	3000 hrs POST	Clinical
Certified Master Social Worker (CMSW)	DSW/MSW	3000 hrs POST	Clinical/Advanced
Certified Social Worker (CSW)	MSW/BSW	None	Not Required

NEVADA

Board of Examiners for Social Workers
4600 Kietzke Lane, Suite C121
Reno, NV 89502
775-688-2555

Title	Education	Experience	AASSWB Exam
Licensed Clinical Social Worker (LCSW)	DSW/MSW	3000 hrs POST	Clinical
Licensed Independent Social Worker (LISW)	DSW/MSW	3000 hrs POST	Advanced
Licensed Social Worker (LSW)	MSW/BSW or MA/BA	None 3000 hrs POST	Basic Basic

NEW HAMPSHIRE

Board of Mental Health Practice
105 Pleasant Street
Concord, NH 03301
603-271-6762

Title	Education	Experience	AASSWB Exam
Certified Clinical Social Worker (CCSW)	DSW/MSW	2 yrs POST	Clinical

NEW JERSEY **State Board of Social Work Examiners**
P. O. Box 45033
Newark, NJ 07101
973-504-6495

Title	Education	Experience	AASSWB Exam
Licensed Clinical Social Worker (LCSW)	DSW/MSW	2 yrs	Clinical
Licensed Social Worker (LSW)	DSW/MSW	None	Intermediate
Certified Social Worker (CSW)	BSW or BA	None 1 yr full-time	Not Required Not Required

NEW MEXICO **Board of Social Work Examiners**
2055 S. Pachoco Street
P. O. Box 25101
Santa Fe, NM 87504
505-476-7100
http://www.state.nm.us

Title	Education	Experience	AASSWB Exam
Licensed Independent Social Worker (LISW)	MSW	2 yrs POST	Clinical/Advanced*
Licensed Master Social Worker (LMSW)	MSW	None	Intermediate*
Licensed Baccalaureate Social Worker (LBSW)	BSW	None	Basic*

*Cultural arts exam also required in New Mexico.

NEW YORK **State Board for Social Work**
New York State Education Department
Cultural Education Center, Room 3041
Albany, NY 12230
518-474-4974
http://www.nysed.gov/prof/csw.htm

Title	Education	Experience	AASSWB Exam
Certified Social Worker (CSW)	MSW	None	Clin/Adv/Interm

NORTH CAROLINA

North Carolina Certification Board for Social Work
103 South Church Street
P. O. Box 1043
Asheboro, NC 27204
335-625-1679
http://www.nccbsw.org

Title	Education	Experience	AASSWB Exam
Certified Clinical Social Worker (CCSW)	DSW/MSW	2 yrs POST	Clinical
Certified Social Work Manager (CSWM)	DSW/MSW/BSW	2 yrs POST	Advanced
Certified Master Social Worker (CMSW)	DSW/MSW	None	Intermediate
Certified Social Worker (CSW)	BSW	None	Basic

NORTH DAKOTA

Board of Social Work Examiners
P.O. Box 914
Bismarck, ND 58502-0914
701-222-0255
http://www.aptnd.com/NDBSWE/

Title	Education	Experience	AASSWB Exam
Licensed Independent Clinical Social Worker (LICSW)	DSW/MSW	4 yrs POST	Clinical
Licensed Certified Social Worker (LCSW)	DSW/MSW	None	Intermediate
Licensed Social Worker (LSW)	BSW	None	Basic

OHIO

Social Work Board
77 South High Street, 16th Floor
Columbus, OH 43266-0340
614-466-0912
http://www.state.oh.us/csw/

Title	Education	Experience	AASSWB Exam
Licensed Independent Social Worker (LISW)	DSW/MSW	2 yrs POST	Clinical/Advanced
Licensed Social Worker (LSW)	DSW/MSW/ BSW	None	Basic
Registered Social Work Assistant (SWA)	AA	None	Not Required

OKLAHOMA

Board of Licensed Social Workers
3535 NW 58th, Suite 765
Oklahoma City, OK 73112
405-946-7230
http://www.state.ok.us/~osblsw

Title	Education	Experience	AASSWB Exam
Licensed for Private Practice (LSW)	DSW/MSW	2 yrs POST	Clinical
Licensed Social Worker (LSW)	DSW/MSW	2 yrs POST	Advanced
Licensed Social Work Assistant (LSWA)	BSW	2 yrs POST	Interm/Basic

OREGON

State Board of Licensed Clinical Social Workers
3218 Pringle Road SE, Suite 240
Salem, OR 97302-6310
503-378-5735
http://bcsw.state.or.us/

Title	Education	Experience	AASSWB Exam
Licensed Clinical Social Worker (LCSW)	MSW	2 yrs POST	Clinical
Clinical Social Work Associate (CSWA)	MSW	None	Not Required

PENNSYLVANIA

State Board for Social Workers, Marriage and Family Therapists, and Professional Counselors
P. O. Box 2649
Harrisburg, PA 17105-2649
717-783-1389
http://www.dos.state.pa.us/bpoa/socwkbd.htm

Title	Education	Experience	AASSWB Exam
Clinical Social Worker (CSW)	DSW/MSW	3 yrs	Clinical

Licensed Social Worker (LSW)	DSW/MSW	None	Intermediate

PUERTO RICO

c/o National Association of Social Workers, Puerto Rico Chapter
271 Ramon Ramos Casellas St.
Urb. Roosevelt
Hata Rey, PR 00918
809-758-3588

Title	Education	Experience	AASSWB Exam
Licensed Social Worker (LSW)	BSW	None	Not Required

RHODE ISLAND

Division of Professional Regulation
Rhode Island Department of Health
3 Capitol Hill, Room 104
Providence, RI 02908-5097
401-277-2827

Title	Education	Experience	AASSWB Exam
Licensed Independent Clinical Social Worker (LICSW)	DSW/MSW	2 yrs POST	Clinical
Licensed Social Worker (LSW)	MSW/BSW	None	Not Required

SOUTH CAROLINA

Board of Social Work Examiners
3600 Forest Drive, Suite 101
P. O. Box 11329
Columbia, SC 29211-1329
803-896-4665
http://www.llr.state.sc.us/bosw.htm

Title	Education	Experience	AASSWB Exam
Licensed Independent Social Worker (LISW)	DSW/MSW	2 yrs POST	Clinical/Advanced
Licensed Master Social Worker (LMSW)	DSW/MSW	None	Intermediate
Licensed Baccalaureate Social Worker (LBSW)	BSW	None	Basic

SOUTH DAKOTA

Board of Social Work Examiners
135 E. Illinois, Suite 214
Spearfish, SD 57783
605-642-1600

Title	Education	Experience	AASSWB Exam
Private Independent Practice (CSW-PIP)	DSW/MSW	2 yrs	Clinical/Advanced
Certified Social Worker (CSW)	DSW/MSW	None	Intermediate
Social Worker (SW)	BSW	None	Basic
	or BA	2 yrs	Basic
Social Work Associate (SWA)	AA/BA	None	Associate

TENNESSEE

Board of Social Work Certification and Licensure
Cordell Hall Building
426 5th Ave. N
Nashville, TN 37247-1010
615-532-5132
http://www.state.tn.us/health/bmf/index.html

Title	Education	Experience	AASSWB Exam
Independent Practitioner (LCSW)	DSW/MSW	2 yrs POST	Clinical
Certified Master Social Worker (CMSW)	DSW/MSW	None	Not Required

TEXAS

State Board of Social Work Examiners
1100 West 49th Street
Austin, TX 78756-3183
512-719-3521
http://www.tdh.state.tx.us/hcqs/plc/lsw.htm

Title	Education	Experience	AASSWB Exam
Advanced Clinical Practitioner (LMSW-ACP)	DSW/MSW	3 yrs POST	Clinical
Advanced Practice (LMSW-AP)	DSW/MSW	3 yrs POST	Advanced
Licensed Master Social Worker (LMSW)	DSW/MSW	None	Intermediate
Licensed Social Worker (LSW)	BSW	None	Basic

Social Work Associate (SWA)*	BA—human sciences or related field	1 yr/3 yrs	Associate

*6 hrs. of continuing education in social work values and ethics must be obtained before the SWA license will be issued.

UTAH

Social Work Licensing Board
Occupational and Professional Licensing
160 East 300 South
P.O. Box 146741
Salt Lake City, UT 84114-6741
801-530-6163

Title	Education	Experience	AASSWB Exam
Clinical Social Worker (CSW)	DSW/MSW	2 yrs POST	Clinical*
Certified Social Worker (CSW)	DSW/MSW	None	Intermediate*
Social Service Worker (SSW)	MSW/BSW or BA	None 1 yr POST	Basic* Basic*

*Law and rules exam also required in Utah.

VERMONT

Office of the Secretary of State
Licensing and Registration Division
109 State Street
Montpelier, VT 05609-1106
802-828-2390

Title	Education	Experience	AASSWB Exam
Licensed Independent Clinical Social Worker (LICSW)	DSW/MSW	2 yrs POST	Clinical

VIRGIN ISLANDS

Board of Social Work Licensure
Number 1 Subbase, 2nd Floor, Room 205
St. Thomas, VI 00802
809-774-3130

Title	Education	Experience	AASSWB Exam
Certified Independent Social Worker (CISW)	DSW/MSW	2 yrs POST	Clin/Adv

Certified Social Worker (CSW)	DSW/MSW	None	Intermediate
Social Worker (SW)	BSW	None	Basic
	or BA	2 yrs POST	Basic
Social Work Associate (SWA)	AA/BA	None	Associate

VIRGINIA

Board of Social Work
6606 West Broad Street, 4th Floor
Richmond, VA 23230-1717
804-662-9914

Title	Education	Experience	AASSWB Exam
Licensed Clinical Social Worker (LCSW)	MSW	2 yrs POST	Clinical
Licensed Social Worker (LSW)	MSW	None	Basic
	or BSW	2 yrs POST	Basic

WASHINGTON

Mental Health Quality Assurance Council
Department of Health Counselors Section
1300 SE Quince
P. O. Box 47869
Olympia, WA 98504-7869
360-236-4900

Title	Education	Experience	AASSWB Exam
Certified Social Worker (CSW)	DSW/MSW	2 yrs POST	Clin/Adv

WEST VIRGINIA

Board of Social Work Examiners
P. O. Box 5459
Charleston, WV 25361
304-558-8816

Title	Education	Experience	AASSWB Exam
Licensed Independent Clinical Social Worker (LICSW)	DSW/MSW	2 yrs POST	Clinical
Licensed Independent Social Worker (LCSW)	DSW/MSW	2 yrs POST	Advanced
Licensed Graduate Social Worker (LGSW)	MSW	None	Intermediate
Licensed Social Worker (LSW)	BSW	None	Basic

WISCONSIN

Board of Social Workers, Marriage & Family Therapists, and Professional Counselors
Department of Regulation and Licensing
P.O. Box 8935
Madison, WI 53708-8935
608-267-7212

Title	Education	Experience	AASSWB Exam
Certified Independent Clinical Social Worker (CICSW)	DSW/MSW	2 yrs POST	Clinical*
Certified Independent Social Worker (CISW)	DSW/MSW	2 yrs POST	Advanced*
Certified Adv. Practice Social Worker (CAPSW)	DSW/MSW	None	Intermediate*
Certified Social Worker (CSW)	MSW/BSW	None	Basic*

*Laws and rules exam also required in Wisconsin.

WYOMING

Mental Health Professions Licensing Board
2020 Carey Avenue, Suite 201
Cheyenne, WY 82002
307-777-7788

Title	Education	Experience	AASSWB Exam
Licensed Certified Social Worker (LCSW)	DSW/MSW	2 yrs POST	Clin/Adv
Certified Social Worker (CSW)	BSW	None	Basic

Appendix E

MSW Application Tracking Sheet

This sheet is provided as a tool to help you organize your application process. Use one tracking sheet for each school to which you apply.

Name of School ______________________________
Address ______________________________
Telephone ______________________________
Fax ______________________________
E-Mail ______________________________
Contact Person ______________________________
Application Deadline ______________________________

Program begins: ❑Fall ❑Winter ❑Spring ❑Summer

Admissions Information Checklist:

Item	***Date Submitted***	***Date of Notice of Receipt by School***
Completed Application	______	______
Letters of reference		
Source	______	______
Source	______	______
Source	______	______
Source	______	______
Source	______	______
Transcripts		
School	______	______
School	______	______
School	______	______
School	______	______

Item	*Date Submitted*	*Date of Notice of Receipt by School*
Standardized Test Results		
Type of Exam ______	______	______
Biographical Statement	______	______
Financial Aid Information		
Free Application for Federal Student Aid (FAFSA)	______	______
State Aid Form (if applicable)	______	______
School Financial Aid Form	______	______
University Financial Aid Form (if applicable)	______	______
Copy of Previous Year's Personal Tax Return	______	______
Copy of Previous Year's Parents' Tax Return (if requested)	______	______

Response from School:

Item	*Date Received*	*Date Returned*
Offer of Admission or Rejection	______	______
Deadline for Acceptance or Rejection of Offer of Admission ___________		
Offer of Financial Aid Award	______	______
Deadline for Acceptance of Offer of Financial Aid Award	______	______
Deposit to Hold Place in Class (Amount: ______)		______
Deadline to Receive a Refund of Deposit (if any)	______	

Appendix F

Making Your Visit Count: Questions to Ask and Things to Look For

I strongly advise that you visit the schools you are seriously considering before you make a final selection of school. The visit can take place either before or after you are offered admission. The advantage to making the visit while your application is still being considered is that you may be able to interview with an admissions person and, in essence, make a case for yourself by the impression you make. As mentioned in Chapter 8, not all schools grant applicants a formal admissions interview. Nevertheless, even in the schools that formally do not make interviews a part of the evaluation process, making a favorable impression during a visit may yield positive results. (Be on your best behavior during the visit, because a negative impression can just as easily have the opposite result!) On the other hand, visiting the school after you are offered admission can also have some advantages. Given that the school has already opened its doors to you, admissions staff may have more of an investment in taking the time to answer many questions. In either event, a visit to a school is an excellent idea, because it will allow you to get a sense of the intangibles that no catalog or video about a school and its community can fully convey.

Some readers may think the checklist that follows is too long, while others may think of items that are not included. It is, of course, not mandatory that you cover all the items posed here. Neither should you limit yourself only to these issues. Rather, they are offered as a starting point in making your own checklist.

1. Make prior arrangements with the admissions office to sit in on classes.

   Class Visits:

   Class _______ Professor _____________ Date and Time _____________

   Class _______ Professor _____________ Date and Time _____________

   Class _______ Professor _____________ Date and Time _____________

2. Make prior arrangements to meet with faculty who are doing work that interests you.

   Professor ________ Date and Time ________ Bldg. and Room ________

   Professor ________ Date and Time ________ Bldg. and Room ________

   Professor ________ Date and Time ________ Bldg. and Room ________

3. Is there knowledgeable and accessible academic advice?

   [ ] Advisors within the school

   [ ] Advisors at the university level (How well do they know social work?)

4. Ask to meet with students from similar backgrounds and circumstances as you.

   Student _________ Date and Time ________ Bldg. & Room __________

   Student _________ Date and Time ________ Bldg. & Room __________

   Student _________ Date and Time ________ Bldg. & Room __________

5. Physical facilities:

   Are the classrooms and seating comfortable? [ ] Yes [ ] No
   Are they adequately heated or cooled? [ ] Yes [ ] No
   How large are typical classes? ________________________________

6. Is the school accessible to the physically disabled? [ ] Yes [ ] No

   What services has the school provided for students with disabilities?

   ____

   ____

7. What provisions does the school (and the university) provide for the safety of students?

Have any students been victims of crimes on campus in the last year?
[ ] Yes [ ] No

If yes, does the university police department provide information about the locations and nature of recent incidents on campus?

____

____

Does the university have van or bus service for students to and from their dormitories and apartments during certain hours of the night?

[ ] Yes If yes, is it free? [ ] Or at what cost? ____________

If you will be living off campus without a car, is there safe and reliable public transportation?

[ ] Yes Cost? ____________

8. Library services:

Does the school have its own library? [ ] Yes [ ] No

If it does...

How well-stocked is it? ____________

Is there a full-time librarian and other qualified staff available during all operating hours? [ ] Yes [ ] No

Is there electronic access to library materials? [ ] Yes [ ] No

If the school does not have its own library...

How well-stocked is the university's main library with social work matter?

____

Are other campus libraries available to you?
[ ] Yes Which? ____________ [ ] No

Does the library have cooperative arrangements with other universities for sharing materials? [ ] Yes [ ] No

If yes, how long does it take to actually receive materials from sister libraries?

____

Do the libraries have state-of-the-art computers that allow you to access materials from other libraries online? [ ] Yes [ ] No

9. Does the school have its own computer center? [ ] Yes [ ] No

   If it does not, is there one at the university? [ ] Yes [ ] No

   Are its hours adequate and accessible to students? [ ] Yes [ ] No

   Is it staffed all of the time or only part of the time by qualified personnel who can answer your questions? [ ] Yes [ ] No

   How current are the computers and related equipment?

   ____

   Are the computers compatible with your personal computer?
   [ ] Yes [ ] No

   Does the university have a computer store with reduced prices to students?
   [ ] Yes [ ] No

   Does the school provide low-interest student loans for the purchase of a computer? [ ] Yes [ ] No

10. Living arrangements:

    Appointments to view dorms and apartments:

    Contact Person __________ Date/Time _____ Bldg. & Room ________

    Contact Person __________ Date/Time _____ Bldg. & Room ________

    What is the range of rental costs? ______________________

    Are utilities included? [ ] Yes [ ] No
    If not, what is the estimated cost? ______________

    Are pets permitted? [ ] Yes [ ] No

    Are the buildings smoke-free? [ ] Yes [ ] No

    Do the buildings and neighborhoods appear safe? ______________

    If you have children, what schools are available? ______________

11. Bookstores:

    How are the prices at the university bookstore? ______________________

    Are there independent cooperative bookstores in the area and how do prices compare? ______________________

12. Health Insurance:

    Is health insurance available through the university? [ ] Yes [ ] No

    Is it required of students to carry health insurance, and is the requirement waived for students who show proof of alternative coverage?
    [ ] Yes [ ] No

13. Eating Facilities:

    Are campus dining facilities reasonable in cost and do you like the food?
    ____

14. Recreational facilities:

    Athletic fields for sports of your choice: ______________________

    Swimming pool: ______________________

    Other activities that interest you: ______________________

15. Community offerings:

    Museums: ______________________

    Concert facilities: ______________________

    Theaters: ______________________

    Other entertainment: ______________________

Appendix G

Biographical Statement Worksheet

The following is one approach that may prove useful in writing your essay. It is important to emphasize that it is not intended as a "recipe" for composing a biographical statement. The task is much too important to think of it as a series of steps that will always lead to a common outcome. Instead, the approach suggested is intended as a tool to help you organize your thoughts.

1. Make a thorough self-assessment of your experiences before writing your statement by making a list of all jobs, including those not directly related to social work:

Employer	*Position*
____________________	______________________________
____________________	______________________________
____________________	______________________________
____________________	______________________________
____________________	______________________________

2. List all internships you have ever held:

Agency/Location	*Position*
____________________	______________________________
____________________	______________________________
____________________	______________________________
____________________	______________________________
____________________	______________________________

3. Once you have a list of all the experiences, look at what you did in each of your positions. Make sure to list every task you had to perform on a daily basis:

Position	*Tasks Performed*
____________	____________
____________	____________
____________	____________
____________	____________
____________	____________

4. Once you've identified each task, list the skills that you needed in order to perform each task.

Task	*Skills Required*
____________	____________
____________	____________
____________	____________
____________	____________
____________	____________

5. Once you've identified the skills, establish a connection to your future goals by identifying how those skills are applicable to social work. The section on social work settings in Chapter 9 of this book discusses social work skills and may help you in this process.

Skill	*Applicability to Social Work*
____________	____________
____________	____________
____________	____________
____________	____________
____________	____________

6. List classes that you've taken that contributed to your understanding of social work skills:

Class	*Skills Identified*
____________________	____________________________
____________________	____________________________
____________________	____________________________
____________________	____________________________
____________________	____________________________

7. Use the list of skills from jobs, internships, and classes to identify the areas of social work where you may want to go in the future. Once again, Chapter 9 of this book can help you in identifying areas of social work practice.

Social Work Skills	*Specific Social Work Area of Practice*
____________________	____________________________
____________________	____________________________
____________________	____________________________
____________________	____________________________
____________________	____________________________

8. Make the connection between your goals (i.e., areas of social work practice that interest you) and the particular school's program.

Settings	*Programs That Train For That Setting*
____________________	____________________________
____________________	____________________________
____________________	____________________________
____________________	____________________________
____________________	____________________________

Completing this worksheet should help you see more clearly how your past experiences have helped you develop skills that are applicable to specific social work areas of practice. That knowledge, in turn, will help you better identify the schools that have programs best suited to prepare you for your goals.

Armed with this knowledge, read carefully Chapters 10 and 11 of this book to help you address the specific points requested by the schools to which you are making application.

Appendix H

For More Information

Books

American Association of State Social Work Boards. (1998). *Social Work Laws and Board Regulations.* Culpeper,VA: Author.

Doelling, Carol Nesslein. (1997). *Social Work Career Development*. Washington, DC: NASW Press.

Ginsberg, Leon. (1998). *Careers in Social Work*. Needham Heights, MA: Allyn and Bacon.

Grant, Gary B., and Grobman, Linda M. (1998). *The Social Worker's Internet Handbook.* Harrisburg, PA: White Hat Communications.

Grobman, Linda M. (Ed.) (1999). *Days in the Lives of Social Workers, 2nd Edition.* Harrisburg, PA: White Hat Communications.

Organizations

American Association of State Social Work Boards (AASSWB)
400 South Ridge Parkway, Suite B
Culpeper, Virginia 22701
800-225-6880 or 540-829-6880
540-829-0142 Fax
http://www.aasswb.org

Council on Social Work Education (CSWE)
1725 Duke Street, Suite 500
Alexandria, VA 22314-3457
703-683-8080
703-683-8099 Fax
http://www.cswe.org

National Association of Social Workers (NASW)
750 First Street, NE, Suite 700
Washington, DC 20002-4241
800-638-8799
http://www.socialworkers.org

Web Sites

Free Application for Federal Student Aid (FAFSA)—
http://www.fafsa.ed.gov/

The New Social Worker Online—http://www.socialworker.com

Peterson's Education Center—http://www.petersons.com

Social Work Access Network (SWAN)—http://www.sc.edu/swan/

Social Work Café—http://www.geocities.com/Heartland/4862/

The Student Guide to Financial Aid—http://www.ed.gov/prog_info/SFA/StudentGuide/

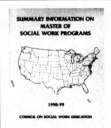

Index

ABOUT THE AUTHOR

Jesús Reyes, AM, ACSW, is a graduate of the School of Social Service Administration (SSA) of the University of Chicago and former Assistant Dean for Enrollment and Placement at SSA. Prior to his administrative work in recruitment, admissions, and job placement at SSA, he practiced social work in a wide variety of settings, including schools, mental health and community settings, health care, and private practice. He is currently Director of Social Service of the Circuit Court of Cook County, Illinois, the largest unified court system in the nation. His Department receives approximately 24,000 court referrals yearly consisting of felony, misdemeanor, ordinance, and traffic violation offenders. With a staff of 260 encompassing 13 court locations, the Department develops and implements an individualized supervision plan for each offender and guides and monitors the offender while he or she remains under the court's supervision. Reyes' broad social work experience, coupled with his experience in admissions at one of the most selective social work programs in the nation, provides a rich source of information for anyone considering entering the profession of social work and applying to graduate social work programs.

DAYS IN THE LIVES OF SOCIAL WORKERS

50 Professionals Tell "Real-Life" Stories from Social Work Practice (2nd Edition)

Edited by Linda May Grobman

"When I read the first story, 'Social Work in the ER,' I found myself saying, 'What an exciting day.' Thank you for your work in bringing not just good stories to print, but a resource for me and others." Delores W. Shirley, MSW, Faculty Liaison/Advisor and Director of Recruitment, University of North Carolina-Chapel Hill School of Social Work

Each chapter is a first-person account written by a professional social worker in a different setting. Readers can take a look at the ups and downs and ins and outs of the writers' real-life days in the "trenches" of social work practice. This book has helped many students decide whether social work is the profession for them, and beyond that, which areas of social work to focus on in their studies and their careers.

Read this book to observe social work practice in the following settings and roles:

- Community and inpatient mental health
- Inner-city and rural schools
- International social work with "raskal" gangs in Papua New Guinea
- Prisons
- Hospitals
- The military
- Managed care
- Residential treatment centers for adolescents
- Homeless outreach
- College counseling centers
- Public child welfare
- Nursing homes
- Hospice
- Adventure-based therapy
- Private practice
- HIV/AIDS research
- Public health
- Administration

....and many more!

This book is an **essential guide** for anyone who wants an inside look at the social work profession. You will learn valuable lessons from the experiences of social workers described in *DAYS IN THE LIVES OF SOCIAL WORKERS, 2nd Edition.*

ISBN: 0-9653653-0-1 1999 Price: $17.95 (U.S.)
Shipping/Handling: $3.50/U.S. addresses; $6/Canada; $12/outside U.S. and Canada

354 pages, 5 ½ x 8 ½ Softcover

Order from White Hat Communications, P.O. Box 5390, Harrisburg, PA 17110-0390 with order form in the back of this book.

THE SOCIAL WORKER'S INTERNET HANDBOOK

by Gary B. Grant and Linda May Grobman

[illegible]

[illegible]

Thousands of social workers are using the Internet [illegible] resources, and [illegible] services and information. You can, too.

Read this book and learn how you can:

- Connect to the Internet
- Choose an Internet Service Provider
- Use mailing lists and newsgroups
- Search the World Wide Web
- [illegible]
- Find [illegible] information and resources for your clients
- [illegible]
- [illegible] funds for your organization or agency using the Internet
- Search online [illegible] social working
- [illegible] Web page

You will also find [illegible]

[illegible]

[illegible]

[illegible]

ORDER FORM

I would like to order the following social work publications from White Hat Communications:

Qty.	Item	Price
_____	Days in the Lives of Social Workers @ $17.95	_____
_____	Social Worker's Internet Handbook @ $24.95	_____
_____	Guide to Selecting/Applying to MSW @ $19.95	_____
_____	New Social Worker Subscription (see page 253)	_____

Please send my order to:

Name ____
Organization ______________________________________
Address ____
City______________________ State____ Zip ______________
Telephone ____

Please send me more information about ❑social work and ❑non-profit management publications available from White Hat Communications.

Sales tax: Please add 6% sales tax for books shipped to Pennsylvania addresses.

Shipping/handling:
❑Books sent to U.S. addresses: $3.50 first book/$1 each add'l book.
❑Books sent to Canada: $6.00 per book.
❑Books sent to addresses outside the U.S. and Canada: $12.00 per book.

Payment:
Check or money order enclosed for $_______
U.S. funds only.

Please charge my: ❑Mastercard ❑Visa
Card #: ____
Name on card: ____________________________________
Billing address (if different from above): ______________
____
Signature: _______________________________________

Mail this form with payment to:

WHITE HAT COMMUNICATIONS, P.O. Box 5390, Dept. GS
Harrisburg, PA 17110-0390
Credit card orders may be called to 717-238-3787
or faxed to 717-238-2090
or order online at http://www.socialworker.com